外语学术核心术语丛书

U0748312

KEY TERMS

IN

LINGUISTICS

语言学核心术语

（英）Howard Jackson　著

蓝　纯　注

外语教学与研究出版社
FOREIGN LANGUAGE TEACHING AND RESEARCH PRESS
北京 BEIJING

京权图字：01-2016-4551

图书在版编目（CIP）数据

语言学核心术语 ：英文、中文 ／（英）霍华德·杰克逊（Howard Jackson）著；蓝纯注． —— 北京 ：外语教学与研究出版社，2016.6（2022.1 重印）
（外语学术核心术语丛书）
书名原文：Key Terms in Linguistics
ISBN 978-7-5135-7772-4

Ⅰ．①语… Ⅱ．①霍… ②蓝… Ⅲ．①语言学－术语－英、汉 Ⅳ．①H0—61

中国版本图书馆 CIP 数据核字（2016）第 152044 号

出 版 人　　王　芳
项目负责　　冯丹丹
责任编辑　　毕　争
封面设计　　孙莉明
版式设计　　吴德胜
出版发行　　外语教学与研究出版社
社　　址　　北京市西三环北路19号（100089）
网　　址　　http://www.fltrp.com
印　　刷　　北京九州迅驰传媒文化有限公司
开　　本　　889×1194　1/32
印　　张　　6.5
版　　次　　2016 年 7 月第 1 版 2022 年 1 月第 7 次印刷
书　　号　　ISBN 978-7-5135-7772-4
定　　价　　29.90 元

购书咨询：（010）88819926　电子邮箱：club@fltrp.com
外研书店：https://waiyants.tmall.com
凡印刷、装订质量问题，请联系我社印制部
联系电话：（010）61207896　电子邮箱：zhijian@fltrp.com
凡侵权、盗版书籍线索，请联系我社法律事务部
举报电话：（010）88817519　电子邮箱：banquan@fltrp.com
物料号：277720101

记载人类文明
沟通世界文化
www.fltrp.com

CONTENTS

总 序

    我国外语教学与研究出版社与国际著名 Bloomsbury 出版集团在 2016 年联合推出了"外语学术核心术语丛书"。本丛书是为初涉各个专业领域的学习者——包括高等院校本科生、硕博士研究生、年轻教师等，特别是外语语言文学专业学习者——准备的专业入门丛书，意义深远。

    本丛书最初由总部设在伦敦的 Continuum 国际出版集团发行，自 2011 年该出版集团隶属于 Bloomsbury 出版集团后，改称 "Bloomsbury Key Terms Series"。经与 Bloomsbury 出版集团商谈后，外语教学与研究出版社结合我国高校情况和需要邀请国内专家撰写导读，并将英语的核心术语译成中文在国内出版。

    "外语学术核心术语丛书"中的"核心术语"意义上不同于英国学者雷蒙·威廉斯（Raymond Williams）在 *Keywords: A Vocabulary of Culture and Society*（1976）一书中的 "keywords"（关键词）。威廉斯所著之书着重考察有关文化和社会的 100 多个关键词在时间长河中的意义和用法变迁，特别是从马克思主义的政治斗争视角进行论述。本丛书的"核心术语"也不同于当今学术期刊文章中出现的"关键词"（key words）。学术期刊文章要求作者在摘要之后列有"关键词"，一般为 3—5 个，每个关键词为 2—6 个字，关注这些核心词的出现频率并便于搜索。与此二者不同，本丛书的编写注重构成某个学科（如哲学或语言学）或理论（如系统功能语言学）的核心术语，为读者提供有关核心词的简易解释和互参方法。这类专业书籍的理论基础为连续体（Continuum）理论，即一个学科或理论与核心词汇构成连续体的关系：一端是某学科或理论，经过精密度的逐步分析后，到达由核心术语组成的另一端。这是因为一个学科或理论的存在必然要通过一定数量的专业性术语来论述，而对一个核心术语的理解，必然要通过它和其他术语的区分与比较，最后在该学科或理论的体系中去理解其意义、功能和价值。也只有在这个基础上，我们才得以初步理解和掌握某学科或理论的整体。这是本丛书与传统专业书籍不同的编写原则。

本丛书的另一特色表现在选题时既注重学科性，也考虑到多学科性和跨学科性。这是学术界对当代知识传授与学科发展的崭新认识。从本丛书已经选定的 14 个选题中，有关哲学的有 2 部，即心智哲学和艺术哲学；有关语言和语言学的有 8 部，即语言学、语义学、句法与句法理论、语用学、系统功能语言学、文体学、话语分析和符号学。此外，也有文学理论、翻译学、伦理学和逻辑学的选题。"外语学术核心术语丛书"的出版目的之一就是为了帮助学生摆脱传统专业的概念，扩大视野，了解学科的多层次的复杂联系。正如束定芳和田臻在《语义学核心术语》导读中指出，语义学是研究自然语言的意义，实际上它涉及语言学、哲学、符号学、逻辑学、心理学等诸多领域的学科。可见非外语专业学生也可阅读本套丛书。

有鉴于此，"外语学术核心术语丛书"的编写框架体现了因材施教和由浅入深的基本原则。为了帮助各个专业的学习者理解和掌握相关学科或理论，本丛书编写体例基本一致，主要包括以下 5 个方面：

（1）引言：参与编写某学科或理论的作者应对该专题的基本内容作浅显介绍和解释，如《心智哲学核心术语》的作者在引言中以清晰、简洁和易懂的方式说明心智哲学与哲学的关系，在此过程中提供有关该学科发展的情境和背景。《语言学核心术语》的作者则在引言中对语音学、音系学、词汇学、句法学和语用学均作了简单介绍，进一步向学生推荐社会语言学、心理语言学、应用语言学、语料库语言学和话语分析等课程内容，最后介绍语言学的主要流派。

（2）核心术语：对某学科或理论认真选择最重要最有密切关系的术语，以引导学生初步了解该学科或理论，如《话语分析核心术语》一书收录了309个术语；《系统功能语言学核心术语》收录了342个术语。这些术语有理论的，也有描述的。对每个术语均提供了精确的定义、出处及其与其他术语的关系。就收词量来说，会出现有些重要词语没有收录的情况，如现代逻辑各分支中的许多重要术语没有出现，对此我同意《逻辑学核心术语》导读作者郝兆宽的解释，"对读者而言这应该是好事，不至于一开始就迷失在海量而且极为技术的细节中"。

（3）重要学者：这一部分的内容主要说明，每个选题除了某专业的核心术语外，还向新入门者提供了与某学科或理论有关的权威学者和理论家。如《话语分析核心术语》一书收录了42位重要学者，其中除话语分析各种理论和方法的代表人物外，还有与话语分析有关的哲学家、社会学家、心理学家、人类学家、认知语言学、语用学家、计算机中介交流研究者、语料库语言学家、法律语言学家等等。他们都在不同方面、不同程度上对话语分析理论的发展有所建树。在具体内容上，选题的编写者介绍了这些权威学者的简历，包括他们的生平、研究方向、代表作品以及对话语分析的主要贡献。

（4）代表性论著：这部分内容是有关某学科或理论的重要论著，如《话语分析核心术语》一书在本部分介绍了24部代表作品，基本上概括了话语分析不同时期、不同领域的研究成果，其目的是引导学生有目的地去直接阅读原著，以便深入学习或研究。

（5）索引：在本套丛书的索引中，出现在核心术语和权威学者这两部分的重要术语和人物均提供了页码，这也是本丛书关注术语与人物互参这一重大原则的体现。

除上述内容外，外研社"外语学术核心术语丛书"与英语原版有所不同，它增加了由中国学者撰写的中文导读，并提供了核心术语的中译文。这些内容不仅仅是用中文复述有关选题的基本内容，而且为中国学生提供了更多的有关该学科或理论的信息。这表现在：

（1）尽管中文版的中文导读与原版的英文引言有相通之处，中国学生经由他们熟悉易懂的中文内容可更方便地进一步阅读、理解和掌握原著。

（2）中文导读提供了英语原著作者的信息，如黄国文和刘明介绍了《话语分析核心术语》一书作者英国兰卡斯特大学语言学教授保罗•贝克（Paul Baker）的生平、研究方向、主要著作等。

（3）中文导读补充了几年前出版的英文原著未谈到的重要情况，又增加了原著出版后的近况，特别是中国学者的科研成果。前者可以束定芳和田臻有关《语义学核心术语》的导读为例，他们在谈到 H. P. 格赖斯（H. P. Grice）于 1948 年演讲中提出的意义理论时，在附注中补充了有关意义的讨论，可参阅格赖斯在 1957 发表于 *The Philosophical Review* 的文章；后者如《符号学核心术语》的导读作者张凌介绍了我国符号学的发展情况。

（4）难能可贵的是我国学者能对有关学科和理论发表自己的观点，供学生参考。如《语言学核心术语》导读作者蓝纯总结了原作者选词的 3 个依据，即多年的从教经验、现有的工具书和编者本人对各领域的熟悉程度。《文学理论核心术语》导读作者张剑对该书与此前出版的威廉斯所著的《关键词：文化与社会的词汇》和 M. H. 亚伯拉姆斯（M. H. Abrams）编辑的《文学术语汇编》两书进行比较。黄国文和陈瑜敏在《系统功能语言学核心术语》一书的导读中指出，在该学派内部对"语法隐喻"（grammatical metaphor）是否包括"语篇隐喻"（textual metaphor）存在着不同观点。

如本序言在开篇时所述，外研社"外语学术核心术语丛书"的出版具有深远意义。除了它具有很高的实用价值外，它是一部让学生按自己兴趣、以自学为主的读物，是为学生攀登知识高峰搭建的平台。我们也会发现，"外语学术核心术语丛书"与已有的专业书籍有所不同。它是教材，又非教材；它是辞书，又非辞书；它是专著，又非专著。在这个意义上，它是外研社引进和推出的一个崭新的语类。考虑到当前我国学术界和教育界正在讨论酝酿高等教育和人才培养的改革，本丛书的出版给高等教育改革指引了一个重要的方向。

胡壮麟
北京大学
2016 年 3 月

导　读

一

　　语言学是关于语言的科学，是以人类语言为对象的一种科学化、系统化的理论研究。语言学拥有漫长的历史，已知最早的对语言的描述性研究可以追溯到公元前四世纪的古印度语法学家波你尼（Pāṇini），他在《波你尼经》（Aṣṭādhyāyī）一书中对梵语的语法体系（包括词根、词干、词尾、前缀、后缀、派生词、复合词等）进行了详尽而科学的分析。现代语言学理论的奠基者一般认为是瑞士语言学家索绪尔（Ferdinand de Saussure），他把言语活动分成"语言"（langue）和"言语"（parole）两个部分，将前者界定为言语活动中不受个人意志的支配、为社会成员所共有的部分，将后者界定为言语活动中受个人意志支配、带有个人发音、用词、造句的特点的部分。索绪尔认为，语言学首先应该关注语言本身的结构系统，这开创了语言学研究结构主义的先河。

　　现代语言学研究根据研究对象可以分为关于语言本身的研究（linguistics of language resources）和与语言相关的跨学科研究（interdisciplinary fields of investigation）两大块（Verschueren 2000）。前者传统上被称为理论语言学，包括语音学、音位学、词法学、句法学、语义学等，对语言的声音、结构（词的结构、句的结构）和意义进行描述和分析；后者传统上被称为应用语言学，是将语言学与某个相关领域相结合而产生的界面研究，包括社会语言学、心理语言学、神经语言学、人类语言学、语言教学等。从研究的视角来看，又可以区分出语用学和认知语言学等（Verschueren 2000），前者是从语言使用的角度来考察语言的各个结构层面，后者则是从认知的角度力图对语言的形式及意义做出整合的分析。

跨越了两千多年的历史，语言学已经发展成为一门完备的、独立的学科，具有极高的系统性、科学性、抽象性等特征，反映在术语上，就是无论理论语言学抑或应用语言学都拥有大量特殊的表达，其中有些专属语言学，比如音位（phoneme）、词素（morpheme）；另一些虽然来自日常语言，却被赋予了特殊的意义，比如认知语言学里的角色/背景（figure/ground）、动体/陆标（trajector/landmark）、框架（frame）和脚本（script）等。这些术语一方面是语言学者从事和呈现自己的研究所不可或缺的，另一方面也对非语言学者阅读语言学文献、了解语言学者的研究制造了不少麻烦。各类致力于向对语言学研究感兴趣的人群介绍语言学术语的工具书由此应运而生。《语言学核心术语》（*Key Terms in Linguistics*）便是其中一本。

二

《语言学核心术语》一书由 Howard Jackson 编撰，2007 年由英国 Continuum 出版社出版。顾名思义，该书是一本语言学工具书，收录的是理论语言学及应用语言学各分支领域的关键术语，并给出了简短释义。全书共分 11 章，分别是：语音学和音位学、语法、语义学和语用学、话语和语篇分析、社会语言学、心理语言学、历史语言学、应用语言学、文体学、语料库语言学以及语言学流派。在每一章里，作者首先给出该章的基本术语的释义（比如，第 1 章的两个基本术语是"语音学"和"音位学"），然后按首字母顺序，列出该章所涉领域的关键术语，并逐一进行解释。

如作者在前言中所指出的，对于这类工具书，首先要解决的问题是如何判断哪些术语应该收录，哪些只能忍痛割爱。作者的依据有两个，一是其三十五年的从教经验，二是现有的其他同类工具书。据我看来，作者还有第三个依据，即他对语言学各领域的熟悉程度：他对相对熟悉的领域（比如语法）收录的术语会相应较多，给出的释义也繁简有度；而对相对不那么熟悉的领域（比如语用学、认知语言学）收录的术语就会有所减省，给出的释义有时会相对含糊。

相较于其他同类工具书，本书具有如下两个显著特征。一是因为本书原版定位的目标读者是语言及语言学专业的新生或者选修语言课程的高中生，所以全书语言非常浅显，作者尽了最大努力，避免在对一个术语的解释中穿插其他的术语，因此即使没有任何语言学背景知识的读者使用此书也不会遇到太多障碍。二是从结构上来看，前面的十章分别介绍一到两个分支领域的术语（比如第 1 章是"语音学和音位学"，第 2 章是"语法"），向读者呈现了一幅完整的语言学研究的共时画面；第 11 章则聚焦"语言学流派"，由于不同的流派大多起源于不同的时间，所以通过这一章读者可以约略窥见一幅语言学研究的历时画卷。共时与历时相叠加，使得这本书虽然篇幅短小，容量却很大。对于国内读者来说，本书不仅适合英语专业本科生、研究生用来学习语言学核心术语，也可供对语言学感兴趣的青年研究者参阅。

下面我们逐章进行介绍。

三

第 1 章共介绍了 88 个 / 对语音学和音位学术语，基本涵盖了这两个学科里最重要和最基础的概念。当然，作者在概念遴选时在语音学和音位学中似乎更侧重前者，而在语音学中又更侧重发音语音学

（articulatory phonetics），虽然作者并未单独列出这一概念本身。作者对列举的每一个概念都进行了简短解释，尤为难得的是，对一些核心概念，作者能用寥寥数语便勾勒出其轮廓和内涵。比如，作者在对"元音"（vowel）进行解释时，特别提到元音的音质由三个参数决定，分别是舌位高低/闭开，发音部位的前、中、后，以及唇形。作者还特别举例说明 /i/ 是扁唇的闭元音和前元音，/ɒ/ 是圆唇的开元音和后元音，而 /ə/ 是扁唇、舌位居中的中元音。再比如，作者在解释"互补分布"（complementary distribution）时，除了说明这一概念是音位学中甄别两个音位变体（allophone）是否归属同一个音位的基础，还特别以 [p] 和 [pʰ] 为例进行了阐释。在这一词条的末尾，作者特别强调其"与'自由变异'（free variation）相对"，以提醒读者注意"互补分布"和"自由变异"之间的关系。作者的这些努力在一定程度上增加了此章的可读性，也给读者把握语音学和音位学的基本脉络提供了帮助。

第 2 章是本书篇幅最长的章节，共介绍了 169 个/对语法术语，基本涵盖了词法和句法领域的主要概念。与第一章一样，作者对列举的每一个概念进行了简短解释，其中很多解释，虽只寥寥数语，却清晰勾勒出相关概念的轮廓和内涵。比如，作者对"词"（word）的解释，只用了六七十个单词，就交代清楚了 word 在句法、书写、词法以及词汇学中的不同涵义；又比如，作者对"主语"（subject）的解释，仍是用很少的篇幅，就说明了 subject 这一功能位置一般由名词词组填充，在句子中表征动作的执行者（agent）、事件的经历者（undergoer）以及思维或情感的感受者（experiencer），一般位于句首，出现在谓语前面，但在疑问句中则会与助动词倒装。另外，有些相对不那么常见的术语在本章中也能找到，为读者的使用提供了方便，比如，"上缀"（suprafix，又作 superfix）和"新古典复合词"（neo-classical compound）。前者指以重读或声调形式体现的词缀，例如，从动词 import /ɪmˈpɔːt/ 变为名词 import /ˈɪmpɔːt/，就是通过将重读从第二个音节移至第一个音节实现的；后者指由两个源自希腊语或拉丁语的构词成分（combining form）构成的复合词，例如，geo + phagy, xeno + phobia。不过，作者对个别概念的释义有循环定义的嫌疑，比如，作者对"动词"（verb）的定义是"A class of words that are used to form verb phrases"（用于构成动词短语的词类）。总体而言，瑕不掩瑜，这一章为读者了解词法学和句法学的基本概念提供了很好的入门知识。

相比前两章，第 3 章内容显得简略，仅介绍了 41 个语义学和语用学的基本概念，遗漏颇多。以语用学为例，一些重要概念，比如"面子"（face）、"规约隐涵"（conventional implicature）、"会话隐涵"（conversational implicature）、关联理论（Relevance Theory）等，都没有囊括，不能不说是一种遗憾。从所涵盖的 41 个概念来看，作者秉承了前两章简约明晰的风格，对有些概念的界定相当精到。比如，在对"反义关系"（antonymy）的阐释中，作者言简意赅地介绍了三种反义关系：级差性反义关系（gradable antonymy）、互补性反义关系（complementary antonymy）和对称性反义关系（converse antonymy），并分别举例说明。又如，对"类指"（generic reference）的界定虽只有寥寥四五十词，却通过"Tigers are ferocious beasts"、"The tiger is a ferocious beast"和"A tiger is a ferocious beast"这三个例句，十分清楚地展示了类指的三种常见形式——名词复数、定冠词 + 名词单数、不定冠词 + 名词单数——值得称道。当然，作者对有些概念的界定有待商榷。比如，"适切条件"（felicity condition），作者指出其包括"准备条件"（preparatory condition）和"诚意条件"（sincerity condition），却漏掉了"一般条件"（general condition）、"内容条件"（content condition）和"核心条件"（essential condition）。又比如，"礼貌"（politeness），作者的界定是"语用学中发展出一些礼貌理论，用于解释会话参与者力求'维护'对方'面子'的方式"（Theories of politeness have been developed in pragmatics to account for ways in which participants in conversation strive to 'maintain' their interlocutor's 'face'），但这很难说是对"礼貌"的界定。再比如，"原型"（prototype），从作者给出的释义看，他力图阐释的似乎是"原型理论"（the theory of prototype），而不是"原型"概念本身。总体而言，此章在一定程度上对于读者把握语义学和语用学的基础概念还是有助益的。

第 4 章介绍了 50 个话语分析和语篇分析领域的基础概念。因为入选的概念数量较少，所以与第 3 章一样，有些重要概念被遗漏。比如，"课段"（transaction）、"回合"（exchange）和"话步"（move）入选，但是"课"（lesson）和"话目"（act）却漏选，但是根据 Sinclair & Coulthard（1975），话语结构模式包括五个层次，即 lesson – transaction – exchange – move – act，作者漏掉最高和最低的两个层次，应该说是一种遗憾。就所涵盖的 50 个概念来看，作者依然以短小的篇幅对其中许多概念做出了精当的界定。比如，"相邻语对"（adjacency pair），作者用寥寥数语，不仅交代了这是会话分析领域的基础概念，而且将其准确地释义为"会话中由两个说话者说出的一个构成语对的话语序列"（a sequence of utterances by two speakers in a conversation that form a matching pair），并进行了举例说明。作者还进一步交代相邻语对中的前一个话语被称为"相邻前对"（first pair part），后一个话语被称为"相邻后对"（second pair part），并指出相邻后对又可区分为"首选"（preferred）后对和非首选（dispreferred）后对，且举例进行了说明。在短短几十词的篇幅里，这样的信息量是难能可贵的。又比如，"普遍—特殊（模式）"（general-particular），这是文本中常见的一种结构模式，作者引用 Hoey（1983），将其进一步分为 generalization-example 和 preview-detail 两个小类，从中我们可以清楚地看到作者以尽可能简洁的语言提供尽可能完备的释义的努力。本章的遗憾是除了收录的概念较少外，还有两个概念与前一章重复，分别是"模糊限制语"（hedge）和"所指／指称"（reference）。这两个概念在语用学和话语分析领域中的涵义基本相当，作者所给的释义也大同小异，重复出现所占的篇幅可以省给未能收录的概念。

第 5 章介绍了社会语言学领域的 55 个基础概念。在语言学的各个分支中，社会语言学因为关注语言与社会之间的关系，是相对具象而有趣的，所以本章所囊括的不少概念也鲜活生动，能够在读者头脑中激活一些有趣的语言现象。比如"高层语／高势语／上层方言"（acrolect）和"低层语／低势语／下层语言"（basilect）——前者指一个社会群体中被尊崇的、享有特权的语言变体（如汉语中的普通话），后者指不被尊崇、没有特权的语言变体（如汉语中的各地方言）；再比如"特权／强势"（prestige）和"隐性声望"（covert prestige）——前者通常指一个社会群体赋予其所认定的标准语以特殊地位，后者指除标准语之外，某种语言变体被某个特定的社会群体所尊崇（比如上海话之于上海人）。本章对有些概念的释义很见功力，比如开篇的"口音"（accent），作者不仅点出既存在地域口音，也存在属于某个社会群体的口音，而且说明对口音的辨析可以在不同的层面展开，大到英国口音和美国口音，小到英国北部口音和英格兰西米德兰兹郡（West Midlands）口音，最后还在十分有限的篇幅里强调了"口音"与"方言"（dialect）的差别。对有些不一定为其他类似工具书收录的概念，作者也给了一席之地，比如观察者悖论（observer's paradox），指美国著名社会语言学家 William Labov 所注意到的语料收集中的一个难题，即研究者的在场不可避免地会导致受试者在一定程度上改变自己的说话方式，甚至可能产生"过度纠正"（hypercorrection）。

不过，作者对某几个概念的释义似可商榷。比如"语言"（language），作者仅指出这是一个很难界定的概念，其与"方言"（dialect）的区别模糊不清，却始终没有说到底何谓语言。再比如，"patois"，作者认为这个术语被用于指称"黑人英语中的土语/土话"，但在实际使用中这一概念的外延要广泛得多。又比如，"言语风格"（speech style），作者对这一概念的释义过于简略，甚至未提及言语风格的渐变所形成的连续体，应该说是一种遗憾。

第6章共收录了45个心理语言学领域的基础概念，并给出了简短释义。作者对其中某些概念的把握十分从容，给出的释义举重若轻。比如，"动物交流"（animal communication），作者用寥寥数行就交代了心理语言学家研究动物交流方式的宗旨及主要内容，并列举了蜜蜂、海豚和鲸鱼的交流方式作为例证，最后还提了一笔一些语言学者教黑猩猩等灵长类动物学习语言的不成功的尝试。又比如，"（语言的）设计特征"（design features），作者除了将其释义为"为所有人类语言共享、但不整体见于任何动物交流体系的一组特征"（a set of a dozen or so characteristics of all human languages not found together in any animal communication system），还以四个重要特征为例进行了说明，即任意性（arbitrariness）、移位性（displacement）、创造性（productivity）和双重性（duality of patterning）。再比如，"记忆"（memory），作者言简意赅地介绍了"工作记忆"（working memory）和长期记忆（long-term memory）的区别，还特别提到了"感觉储存"（sensory store）。

不过，作者并非对所有概念都处理得这么游刃有余，有些概念的释义显得语焉不详。比如，"口误"（slips of the tongue），作者仅指出口误为心理语言学家研究言语产出过程提供了证据，却并未直接释义究竟何为口误；又比如，"思维与语言"（thought and language）词条，作者将"思维"和"语言"这两个概念并在一起作为一个词条处理比较奇怪。如果说作者意在强调思维与语言的关系，那么不妨明言两者的关系究竟是什么，但是从作者的释义来看，他对心理语言学领域对思维与语言的关系所做的研究并没有做出成熟妥当的概括。同样的问题也见于"普遍语法"（universal grammar），作者如果能多用一点笔墨例举究竟有哪些语法特征被写进人类的大脑，也许能够帮助读者更好地理解这一概念。

最后，本章的"原型"（prototype）概念在第三章已出现，释义也大同小异。

第 7 章共收录了 36 个历史语言学概念，为前面七章里收录概念最少的一章。虽然收录的概念不多，但有几个却很有特点。比如，"民族语言网"（ethnologue），这是一个与历史语言学研究相关的网站，网址是 http://www.ethnologue.com，这也是本书收录的第一个网站名。又比如，介绍了"威廉·琼斯爵士"（Sir William Jones），他在印度担任法官期间，用业余时间学习东方语言，注意到梵语、希腊语、拉丁语、日耳曼语、凯尔特语等语言之间的同族关系，是最早提出印欧语假说的英国东方学家和语言学家，也是历史比较语言学的奠基人。这也是本书收录的第一个人名。

作者言简意赅的释义风格在"语义变化"（semantic change）这一概念的解释中有充分的体现。在有限的篇幅里，作者用 meat、clerk、knight 和 propaganda 为例，分别介绍了语义的缩小、拓宽、褒化和贬化现象，对于读者理解这一概念很有帮助。

第 8 章是迄今篇幅最短的一章，仅收录了 28 个应用语言学领域的基础概念。考虑到应用语言学研究在最近几十年的突飞猛进和日益重要的影响，作者的这一处理不能不说稍显遗憾。让人印象深刻的概念释义有"中介语 / 语际语 / 过渡语"（interlanguage），作者介绍这一概念最早由 Larry Selinker 提出，指的是在第二语言的习得过程中，学习者在目的语输入的基础上所形成的一种既不同于其第一语言、也不同于其目标语、但随着学习的进展逐渐向目标语过渡的动态的语言系统，最后还不忘交代对学习者中介语的研究能够帮助教师更好地理解学习者在语言习得过程中可能经历的阶段。另外一个言简意赅的概念释义是"词典学"（lexicography），作者将其界定为将语言学的研究成果用于词典编撰、研究按什么范围收词、按什么原则释义和以什么为目的编辑词典的学科，并提及在 20 世纪 60 年代现代语言学迅猛发展之前，词典学已拥有自己漫长的、独立于语言学研究的历史。作者最后还提供了一部参考书 Hartmann & James（2001）。

此章中有些概念的释义有待商榷。比如"计算语言学"（computational linguistics），作者近乎草率地让读者"参考'自然语言处理'"（See 'natural language processing'），但正如作者在"自然语言处理"的释义中所指出的，"计算语言学"并不等同于"自然语言处理"，前者比后者的范围更广。又比如"语言意识"（language awareness），作者的释义是"促进并提升对语言的理解，包括语言的教与学"（promoting and raising understanding of language and languages, including the teaching and learning of and about language (s)），但这与其说是解释"语言意识"，毋宁说是解释"提升语言意识"。再比如，"少数族群权利"（minority rights），作者仅指出"在语言规划和政策中，语言学可被用于解决说少数语言的言语群体所面临的问题"（in the context of language planning and policy, linguistics can be applied to the problems of speech communities that speak a minority language），但并未解释究竟何为"少数族群权利"。同样的问题也见于"动机 / 态度"（motivation/attitude），作者仅指出它们对于二语学习十分重要，却并未说明究竟什么是"动机"，什么是"态度"。

第 9 章收录了 36 个 / 对文体学常用概念。且举几例来赏析作者言简意赅的风格。首先，"语场 / 语旨 / 语式"（field/tenor/mode），作者将这三个概念放在一个词条中处理是经过斟酌的，因为它们都是 Halliday（1973）所提出的"语域理论"（register theory）的一部分，其中，"语场"指文本的主题内容，"语旨"即文本的产出和接收过程中各参与者及其之间的关系，"语式"指文本的交流方式，比如是口头的还是笔头的。其次，"前景化"（foregrounding），作者将其界定为"借自艺术批评的术语，指使用风格策略突出文本中的特定部分"（a term taken from art criticism to refer to the use of stylistic devices to give prominence to certain aspects of a text）。但作者没有止步于此，而是进一步举例说明最简单的前景化可以通过大号或黑体字体以及下划线等手段来实现，但更主要的是通过语法、词汇或语义上的"偏离"（deviance）来实现，还可通过排比句式实现。第三，"叙事角度 / 视角"（point of view），作者解释在叙事性文本中，叙述者都是从某种特定的视角来讲述故事，并且文本作者可以征用不同的叙述者从各自的视角来展开讲述；总体而言，可以区分第一人称视角和第三人称视角，而叙述者可以置身于故事外，也可以处在故事中。

第 10 章虽然只收录了 39 个语料库语言学的基础概念，但是作者尽其所能提供了很多信息。比如，作者介绍了六个著名的英语语料库：柯林斯英语语料库（Bank of English）、英国国家语料库（British National Corpus）、现代和中世纪英语国际计算机档案（ICAME）、国际英语语料库 / 英语国际语料库（International Corpus of English）、兰卡斯特—奥斯陆 / 卑尔根语料库（LOB）和牛津英语语料库（Oxford English Corpus），并一一给出了网址。此外，作者还介绍了多种不同类型的语料库：平衡语料库（balanced corpus）、历史语料库（historical corpus）、动态监察语料库（monitor corpus）、平行语料库（parallel corpus）、句法标注语料库（parsed corpus）、词性标注语料库（tagged corpus）、样本语料库（sample corpus）、全文语料库（full-text corpus）以及树图语料库（Treebank）。这些信息对读者进入语料库语言学这一方兴未艾的领域大有助益。

第 11 章共收录了 79 个概念，涵盖了结构主义（structuralism）、系统功能语言学（systematic-functional linguistics）、转换生成语法（transformational generative grammar）、依存语法（dependency grammar）和认知语言学（cognitive linguistics）等五大流派，其中结构主义又分为索绪尔派和布龙菲尔德派。如果说前面十章是从理论语言学及应用语言学的十个分支来分述的话，那么这最后一章就是从语言学的五大流派入手，梳理各流派的核心概念。两相结合，使得全书对语言学的基础和重要概念的呈现更加完整。

当然，在最后一章中，作者并非对所有概念的把握都那么精准。以认知语言学（cognitive linguistics）为例，作者对"认知语言学"这一概念本身，以及"认知语法"（cognitive grammar）、"概念隐喻"（conceptual metaphor）、"理想化认知模型"（idealized cognitive model）和"意象图式"（image schema）等概念的释义都显得有些语焉不详，未能抓住最关键的内容。比如，作者对"认知语法"的释义是"旨在为语言体系建模，即'心智语法'。意义被视为在语法中占据中心位置，语言被视为整合的而非模块的"（This aims to model the language system, the 'mental grammar'. Meaning is seen as central to grammar, and language is not conceived as modular but as integrated），就显得过于简略而不得要领。又比如，"概念隐喻"，作者的释义只有一句"思维被认为在本质上是隐喻性的"（Thought is said to be fundamentally metaphorical），也很难说完整地抓住了这一概念的主要内涵。再比如，"理想化认知模型"，作者如果能在释义中举一两个经典的例子（像他对其他一些概念的处理一样），那么他的解释就会更有说服力，对读者的帮助也会更大。

　　总体而言，作者以"语言学流派"收束全书，很好地提升了本书所收录概念的完整性和代表性，也有助于读者从一个宏观的角度梳理自己的语言学知识。

参考书目

Halliday, M. A. K. (1973) *Explorations in the Functions of Language*, London: Edward Arnold.

Hartmann, R. R. K. & James, G. (2001) *Dictionary of Lexicography*, London: Taylor & Francis Ltd.

Hoey, M. (1983) *On the Surface of Discourse*, London: George Allen and Unwin.

Sinclair, J. & Coulthard, R. (1975) *Towards an Analysis of Discourse: The English Used by Teachers and Pupils*, Oxford: Oxford University Press.

Verschueren, J. (2000) *Understanding Pragmatics*, Beijing: Foreign Language Teaching and Research Press.

蓝纯

北京外国语大学

Preface

Inevitably with a publication of this kind, the selection of terms to be included will be the personal choice of the author. In this case, it is based both on my experience of teaching about language for over thirty-five years, and on my perusal of other works of a similar nature. The latter has been necessary especially where my expertise is limited, since no linguist has a detailed knowledge of all the areas of language study.

The terms have been selected with the beginning student of language or linguistics in mind, perhaps undertaking one of the GCE A-level courses in the English language, or in the first year or so of a degree course in linguistics, the English language, or a modern language.

Rather than being presented in a straight alphabetical list, the terms have been arranged under headings representing the traditional divisions of linguistics, and which may correspond to modules or courses that you are studying. The largest of these sections is for grammar (morphology and syntax), which reflects both the centrality of this part of linguistics and the fact that many of the other linguistic disciplines depend on and extensively use the terms of grammar in their own studies.

There is an alphabetical index at the end, in case you cannot readily find the term you are looking for; and there are extensive cross-references in the entries (in **bold**), so that you can see how terms are related to each other.

A reference work of this kind cannot expect to be comprehensive. The hope is that you will not be disappointed by not finding the term you are looking for. If this is the case, however, please inform me, via the publishers, so that the term can be included in any subsequent edition.

Phonetics and phonology

Phonetics 语音学

The study of speech sounds, the use that the human voice makes of the sounds it can produce for the purposes of speaking. Speech sounds can be studied from the perspective of how they are produced by the human vocal organs; this is called 'articulatory phonetics'. They may also be studied from the perspective of the physical attributes of their sound; this is known as 'acoustic phonetics', or 'instrumental phonetics', since an array of instruments or machines is used to measure sound qualities. Besides the study of sound segments (phones), phonetics also studies the use that the human voice makes of pitch and tone, both in speaking individual words (as in **tone languages**) and over longer utterances (as in **intonation**).

Phonology 音系学 / 音位学

The study of how speech sounds are used in a language to form syllables and words and to make differences of meaning. It studies the sounds (**phonemes**) that a language uses, classifies them (the phoneme inventory), examines their systematic variation (**allophones**), and considers the role of tone and pitch in conveying meaning. Some linguists draw a sharp distinction between phonetics (the study of human speech) and phonology (the use made by a particular language of human speech possibilities); but others see the difference as more about level of detail, so that it is quite legitimate to talk of 'English phonetics and phonology' (Roach 2000).

Accent 口音 / 重音

Sometimes used for **stress**. See also the Sociolinguistics section.

Acoustic phonetics 声学语音学

The branch of phonetics that treats speech sounds from the perspective of their physical properties; also sometimes called 'instrumental phonetics', because the properties of speech sounds are studied with the aid of instruments such as a spectrograph.

Affricate 塞擦音

A **consonant** sound, beginning with a **plosive** closure, but concluding with a **fricative** release. English has two affricate sounds: /tʃ/ initially and finally in <u>church</u>; /dʒ/ initially and finally in <u>judge</u>.

(Allo)phone 音位变体 / 同位音

The (variant) phonetic realization(s) of a **phoneme**. For example, the /l/ phoneme in English has a 'clear' allophone [l] before vowels (<u>leak</u>), a 'dark' (velarized) allophone [ɫ] at the end of words (<u>keel</u>), and a devoiced allophone [l̥]after voiceless plosives (<u>plain</u>). Note that phonemes are written between slash brackets / /, and (allo)phones between square brackets [ ]; see **transcription**.

Alveolar 齿龈 / 齿龈音 / 齿槽音

A consonant sound produced by contact or near-contact of the tongue tip and the alveolar ridge, located just behind the gums of the upper front teeth. Alveolar sounds in English include: /t d s z l/.

Apical 舌尖音

A sound made using the tip of the tongue as the active **articulator**.

Approximant 近音 / 通音

A sound produced by bringing **articulator**s towards each other but without constriction of the airstream. Their articulation is more like that of vowels (hence their alternative label of 'semi-vowel'), but they operate as consonants in the structure of **syllable**s. The approximants used in English are /w/ (well), /j/ (yell), /r/ (real).

Articulator 发音器官

The parts of the mouth (vocal tract) that are used in making speech sounds; a distinction is made between an 'active' articulator, especially the tongue, which moves, and a 'passive' articulator, such as the roof of the mouth, which is stationary.

Aspiration 送气

The puff of air that may accompany the articulation of **plosive** consonants, e.g. in English when an unvoiced plosive occurs before a vowel, as in pin, ten, king. It is indicated phonetically by a superscript 'h', e.g. [pʰɪn].

Assimilation 同化

The movement of one sound to the **place** or **manner of articulation** of an adjacent sound. In 'regressive' assimilation, a following sound influences a preceding one, e.g. in bad boys the /d/ of bad assimilates to the **bilabial** articulation of the /b/ of boys, to give /bæb bɔɪz/. In 'progressive' assimilation, a preceding sound influences a following one, e.g. in this day, the /d/ of day becomes **devoice**d under the influence of the voiceless /s/ at the end of this.

Bilabial 双唇音

A sound produced using the two (bi) lips (labia), e.g. /p b m/.

Cardinal vowels 基本元音 / 主要元音 / 正则元音

A system developed by the phonetician Daniel Jones (1881-1967) for charting the vowel sounds of a language on the basis of their auditory quality. The first eight (primary) cardinal vowels are the front vowels /i e ɛ a/ and the back vowels /u o ɔ ɑ/. The next eight (secondary) cardinal vowels are the rounded/unrounded counterparts to the first eight: /y ø œ ɶ/ for the front ones, and /ɯ ɤ ʌ ɒ/ for the back ones.

Click 吸气音

A sound formed by an intake of air into the mouth, which is closed off at the hard palate (**velum**). Clicks are included in the **phoneme** inventory of some southern African languages, e.g. Xhosa. Non-speech clicks would include a kiss and the sound represented by tsk tsk or tut tut.

Coarticulation 协同发音

Where the articulation of two adjacent sounds overlap, e.g. in the pronunciation of swoon, the lips are already rounded for /s/ (not normally part of its articulation, e.g. sleep) in anticipation of the articulation of /w/ and /uː/.

Complementary distribution 互补分布

In phonology, the basis for assigning two (**allo**)**phones** to the same **phoneme**, because their distribution does not overlap (i.e. is complementary). For example, [p] and aspirated [pʰ] do not occur in the same environments (or create a **minimal pair**); [p] but not [pʰ] occurs after /s/, and [pʰ] occurs elsewhere (e.g. word-initially and word-finally); so [p] and [pʰ] are in complementary distribution and, because they are phonetically similar, they are regarded as allophones of the same phoneme. Compare **free variation**.

Consonant 辅音

A class of sounds that are articulated with some impediment to the airflow through the mouth and that function in the margins of **syllables**. Consonants are further subclassified according to the nature of the obstruction to the airflow: **plosive, fricative, affricate, lateral, nasal.**

Dark 'l' 浑浊 / 暗音 'l'   dear 'l' 清晰 / 明音 'l'

The /l/ in <u>leap</u> is a clear 'l', that in <u>peal</u> is dark, or 'velarized', articulated with the back of the tongue drawn up towards the **velum**. Clear 'l' is symbolized by /l/, and dark 'l' by [ɫ]. Clear and dark 'l' are in **complementary distribution** in English.

Dental 齿音

A sound produced by contact or near-contact of the tongue tip with the back of the upper front teeth. Dental sounds in English are: /θ/(<u>**thin**</u>), /ð/(<u>**then**</u>). In some languages, sounds like /t d n/ are dental rather than alveolar as in English.

Devoicing （浊音）清化

When a **voiced** sound loses some or all of its voicing. For example, voiced plosives at the end of words in German are often devoiced (<u>Rad</u> 'wheel' is pronounced /rɑt/); in English a voiced consonant at the beginning of a word may be devoiced under the influence (**assimilation**) of a preceding voiceless consonant (<u>nice game</u> is pronounced /naɪs keɪm/).

Diacritic 变音符号 / 附加符号

In phonetic **transcription**, a small mark above or below a symbol to indicate some modification, such as a **secondary articulation**; e.g. the diacritic / ̫ / indicates lip rounding, so [s̫] would indicate /s/ pronounced with **rounded** lips.

Diphthong 双元音 / 二合元音

A vowel sound that involves a glide from one 'pure' vowel (monophthong) to another. In English, diphthongs tend towards either /ɪ/ (make /eɪ/), or /ʊ/ (found /aʊ/), or /ə/ (pure /ʊə/).

Distinctive feature 区别特征

A component of a sound that serves to distinguish phonemes from each other. A phoneme may be viewed as a bundle of distinctive features, expressed either in articulatory or in acoustic terms; e.g. /p/ is a voiceless (– voice), bilabial (+ labial), plosive (+ stop), consonant (+ consonant). It is suggested that a small number (around twelve) of distinctive features can serve to describe the speech sounds in every language.

Elision 省略 / 省音

The omission of a sound, especially as occasioned by the phonetic environment; e.g. in clusters of three consonants at word boundaries in English, where the middle consonant is /t/ or /d/, it is likely to be subject to elision, as in slept badly /slep bædli/.

Flap/tap 闪音 / 触音

The terms are now used interchangeably – a single strike of the tongue, usually against the **alveolar** ridge, e.g. in the American pronunciation of /t/ in words like matter /mæɾər/. A flap is distinguished from a 'trill', which involves repeated taps; compare Spanish pero 'but' (with a tap) from perro 'dog' (with a trill).

Formant 共振峰

In **acoustic phonetics**, relating to the 'frequency' of speech sounds, especially vowels; a formant is a peak in such frequency, determined by the position of the tongue in the mouth. Three formants are usually distinguished for each vowel sound, and they can be charted by means of a spectrograph.

Fortis 强（辅）音　　lenis 弱（辅）音

The terms mean 'strong' / 'weak' and are applied to consonant sounds; they refer to the force with which a consonant is articulated. In English, the voiceless plosives /p t k/ are fortis consonants, whereas the voiced plosives /b d g/ are lenis consonants.

Free variation 自由变异

When two sounds may occur in the same environment without making a **minimal pair** or causing a change of meaning, e.g. substituting a glottal stop [ʔ] for /t/ at the end of <u>but</u>.

Fricative 擦音 / 摩擦音

A consonant sound formed by **articulator**s coming close together and friction occurring as the airstream is forced through the narrow gap. Fricatives in English include the initial sounds of: <u>fine</u>, <u>vine</u>; <u>thin</u>, <u>then</u>; <u>sink</u>, <u>zinc</u>; <u>sheet</u>, <u>gite</u> – represented by the phonetic symbols /f v θ ð s z ʃ ʒ/.

Glide 滑音

An **approximant**, e.g. /j w/, that eases the transition between two vowels, especially at word boundaries, e.g. in <u>blue eyes</u> /blʊ w aɪz/. This is an example of an 'off-glide', where the glide /w/ follows from the /u/ of <u>blue</u>. An 'on-glide' anticipates the following vowel, as in <u>tie it</u> /taɪ j ɪt/.

Glottal 声门音 / 喉音

Sound produced in the **glottis**, such as /h/ (hit) and the glottal stop /ʔ/, which substitutes for /t/ in some (e.g. London Cockney) pronunciations of words like <u>butter</u>.

Glottis 声门

Located in the larynx, the glottis is the site of the **vocal cords**. The 'state of the glottis' influences the quality of the speech sounds that are produced, e.g. whisper, creaky voice. In particular, whether the vocal cords are vibrating or not determines whether the sound is **voiced** or unvoiced.

Homorganic 同部位的 / 同部位音

Sounds made at the same place of articulation, e.g. in <u>sing carols</u>, the final sound of <u>sing</u> /ŋ/ and the initial sound of <u>carols</u> /k/ are homorganic, both being **velar** articulations.

Intervocalic 元音间（辅音）

Used of consonants that occur between vowels, e.g. /t/ is intervocalic in <u>sitting</u> /sɪtɪŋ/.

Intonation 语调

The variations in pitch that accompany speech and serve to organize it into **tone unit**s (information units). Intonation may distinguish between sentence types, e.g. statement, polar question, content question. It may also serve to express the speaker's attitude and emotional state, e.g. aggression, irritation, acquiescence.

Intrusive 'r' （元音间的）插音 'r'

A case of **liaison**, where an 'r' is inserted between vowels at word boundaries, even though one is not present in the spelling, e.g. in <u>law and order</u>. /lɔː r ænd ɔːdə/. Compare **linking 'r'**.

IPA (International Phonetic Alphabet) 国际音标

Invented in the late nineteenth century to provide a set of symbols that would represent the sounds of the world's languages on the basis of 'one symbol per sound'. The IPA is widely used by field linguists and language teachers, and it is now the standard method for representing pronunciation in dictionaries, at least in the UK. For more information, see the website of the International Phonetic Association: http://www. arts.gla.ac.uk/IPA/ipa.html.

Labialization 唇音化 / 圆唇化

A **secondary articulation** involving lip rounding, e.g. in the articulation of /t/ in <u>tool</u> [tuːɫ], anticipating the lip rounding of /uː/.

Labio-dental 唇齿音

A sound produced with the bottom lip and the top teeth, e.g. /f/ (<u>foot</u>), /v/ (<u>vote</u>).

Lateral 边音 / 边音性

A speech sound made with the tongue in contact with the roof of the mouth and the air allowed to escape over the sides of the tongue, i.e. laterally. Lateral sounds are types of /l/, including the lateral fricative /ɬ/, where the sides of the tongue are raised so that friction occurs as the air escapes between the tongue and the gums/teeth. The lateral fricative occurs in Welsh, represented by 'll' in spelling, e.g. in the word for 'lake', <u>llyn</u>.

Liaison 连音 / 连续增音

The insertion of a sound at the end of a word to ease the transition to the pronunciation of the following word. For example, French <u>nos</u> 'our' is pronounced in isolation with the 's' silent /no/; however, when <u>nos</u> is followed by a word beginning with a vowel, liaison takes place and the 's' is pronounced, e.g. <u>nos amis</u> 'our friends' /noz ami/.

Linking 'r' 连接音 / 连系音 'r'

A case of **liaison**, where, for a particular accent, the 'r' in words like *far* is not pronounced, except as a linkage to a following word beginning with a vowel, e.g. <u>far away</u> /fɑː r əweɪ/. Compare **intrusive 'r'**.

Liquid 流音

A group of sounds that includes 'r' and 'l' sounds, made with the tongue tip (**apical**) against the **alveolar** ridge.

Manner of articulation 发音方式

This refers to the type of constriction to the airstream in the articulation of consonants. Complete constriction occurs with **plosive**s, also called stops. Complete constriction, together with escape of air through the nose, occurs with **nasal**s. Complete constriction, together with escape of air over the sides of the tongue, occurs with **lateral**s. Partial constriction, together with friction, occurs with **fricative**s. Little or no constriction occurs with **approximant**s, also called semi-vowels.

Metathesis （两个相邻音的）换位 / 易位 / 语音换位

The reversal of two sounds, e.g. where <u>ask</u> becomes <u>aks</u> in some dialects of English.

Minimal pair 最小对立对

A pair of words that differ by a single **phoneme**, and have different meanings, used to establish that the sounds in question are separate phonemes of the language. For example, <u>pump/bump</u> are a minimal pair, to establish that /p/ and /b/ are separate phonemes in English.

Nasal 鼻音

A manner of articulation that involves a constriction in the mouth, but the escape of air through the nose. In English, the following nasal sounds occur: bilabial /m/ (<u>mist</u>), alveolar /n/ (<u>nest</u>), velar /ŋ/ (sti<u>ng</u>). A labio-dental nasal /ɱ/may be heard as an allophone of /m/ before /f/, e.g. in <u>comfort</u>, <u>symphony</u>. Compare **oral**.

Neutralization 中和化 / 中和作用

In an environment where a **phonem**ic distinction that applies elsewhere no longer does. For example, the distinction between **voiced** and unvoiced plosives (/b d g/ vs /p t k/) is neutralized after /s/ in English: the unaspirated voiceless plosive occurs (<u>spin</u>, <u>stint</u>, <u>skin</u>), but the voiced one does not (no /sb sd sg/).

Nucleus 音节核，调核

The core **phoneme** of a **syllable**, usually a vowel, which may be preceded by an 'onset' and followed by a 'coda', both containing consonants. For example, in the syllable <u>black</u> /blæk/, the nucleus is the vowel /æ/. The term 'nucleus' is also used in **intonation**, to denote the syllable within a **tone unit** on which the main pitch movement occurs.

Obstruent 阻塞音

A speech sound formed by some obstruction or constriction in the mouth, either complete (as with **plosives**) or partial, producing friction (as with **fricatives**). Besides plosives and fricatives, the other class of obstruent sounds is that of **affricates**. Compare **sonorant**.

Oral 口腔音（与鼻音相对）

A sound made wholly in the mouth (vocal cavity), rather than using the nasal cavity; any sound that is not a **nasal**.

Palatal 腭音 / 上腭音 / 硬腭音 / 舌面中音

A sound formed by the blade of the tongue having contact or near-contact with the hard palate (roof of the mouth). The only palatal sound in English is the **approximant** /j/ (<u>yell</u>). In Spanish, the letters 'll' represent a palatal **lateral**, as in <u>llave</u> 'key', and the letter 'ñ' represents a palatal **nasal** /ɲ/, as in <u>mañana</u> 'tomorrow'.

Palato-alveolar 腭龈音

A sound (only **fricatives**) made with the tongue tip in near-contact with the alveolar ridge and the tongue blade drawn towards the palate. Also called 'post-alveolar', these sounds are, in English: /ʃ/ (<u>ship</u>) and /ʒ/ (<u>leisure</u>).

Paralinguistic 副语言（特征）/ 辅助语言（特征）

Features of speech that are not strictly linguistic, such as loudness, voice quality (e.g. as a result of having a cold), pitch variation that is not part of intonation (e.g. high pitch caused by excitement).

Pharyngeal 咽音

A consonant sound articulated by the root of the tongue drawn to the back wall of the pharynx; they occur, for example, in Semitic languages such as Arabic.

Phonation 发声（态）

What takes place in the larynx, particularly in relation to the vocal cords. Types of phonation, besides voicing, include 'creaky voice', 'breathy voice' and whisper.

Phoneme 音位

A sound segment in a language. One task of **phonology** is to establish the phonemes of a language. The phonemes are the contrastive sounds of a language, such that the substitution of one phoneme for another causes a change of word or meaning. A phoneme may have a number of 'realizations', or **allophone**s, which may be in **complementary distribution** or in **free variation**. Alphabetic writing systems are attempts to symbolize at the level of phonemes (compare syllabic and logographic systems); however, English has 26 letters, but around 44 phonemes, so the relationship between sound and letter is not one-to-one.

Phonotactics 音位排列／音位组合／语音配列／音位结构学

This specifies the permissible phoneme combinations in a language, e.g. the possible consonant clusters in the onset and coda of a **syllable**.

Place of articulation 发音部位

This refers to the **articulator**s used in making consonant sounds, i.e. where in the vocal tract (mouth) the contact or near-contact of articulators takes place. The main places of articulation are, starting at the front of the mouth: bilabial (two lips), labio-dental (bottom lip + top teeth), dental (tongue tip + top teeth), alveolar (tongue tip + alveolar ridge), palatal (tongue blade + hard palate), velar (back of tongue + soft palate/velum), uvular (back of tongue + uvula), glottal (in the glottis).

Plosive 破裂音 / 塞音 / 爆破音

A consonant sound made with a complete constriction of the airstream in the mouth, followed by the release of the air causing 'plosion'. Sometimes the plosion is accompanied by aspiration, as with the unvoiced plosives in English, except after /s/: compare <u>pin</u> [pʰɪn], where /p/ is aspirated, and <u>spin</u> [spɪn], where it is unaspirated. There are three pairs of unvoiced/voiced plosives in English: bilabial /p b/, alveolar /t d/, velar /k g/. Plosives are also called 'stops'; this label derives from the stopping of the airstream behind a constriction. In some contexts, plosives are 'unreleased', e.g. in <u>sit down</u>, the /t/ of <u>sit</u> is not normally released, because the articulation proceeds straight to the following /d/, which is **homorganic** with it.

Prosody 韵律

This is used variously to refer to features of speech that relate to more than a single segment (phoneme). Traditionally, it refers to the patterns of **stress** and **intonation** that occur in speech. It is also used to refer to the structure of syllables, as well as to features that may accompany a syllable, e.g. the feature of nasality that accompanies a word like <u>man</u>, so that the whole syllable/word is characterized by nasality, including the vowel, because the initial and final consonant are both nasal (the nose is not blocked off at all during the articulation of <u>man</u>).

Reduced form 弱读形式 / 弱化形式

The form of a function word in connected speech, when the vowel has been reduced to **schwa** and phonemes have been elided. For example,

<u>and</u> in its full form is pronounced /ænd/, but it is often reduced to /ənd/ or /ən/, or even /n/; similarly <u>have</u> /hæv/ is reduced to /həv/, /əv/, or /v/.

Retroflex 卷舌音

A consonant sound formed by curling the tip of the tongue behind the alveolar ridge. Retroflex consonants may be plosives, fricatives, nasals, laterals, or approximants. Retroflex consonants may be voiced or unvoiced, and retroflex plosives may be aspirated or unaspirated. They are common in languages in the north of the Indian subcontinent, e.g. Panjabi, Gujerati, Bengali, Hindi/Urdu. The IPA symbols for retroflex consonants are similar to those for alveolar consonants, but with a tail, e.g. /ʈ ʂ ɳ/.

Rhotic 带 r 音的 / r 音化的

An **accent** of English in which the 'r' of spelling is pronounced when it comes after a vowel or before a consonant, and not just before a vowel, e.g. in words like <u>far</u>, <u>cart</u> and not just in <u>red</u>. The /r/ phoneme is pronounced in a wide variety of ways by speakers of English.

Rounding 圆唇 / 圆唇性

The formation of the lips when articulating a vowel sound. Vowels may be rounded, with the lips made round, as in /u/ <u>boot</u>, or /ɔ/ in <u>bought</u>. Vowels may be unrounded, with the lips spread, as in /i/ <u>beat</u>, or /e/ <u>bet</u>. In English, front vowels /i e æ/ tend to be unrounded and back vowels /u ɔ ɒ/ rounded. Rounded front vowels occur in French, e.g. <u>tu</u> /ty/, and in German, e.g. <u>Söhne</u> /zønə/ 'sons'.

Schwa 央元音 / 央音性

The neutral sounding vowel, symbolised by /ə/, which is the most common vowel in unstressed syllables in English, e.g. at the beginning of <u>about</u> /əbaʊt/ and at the end of <u>later</u> /leɪtə/.

Secondary articulation 次发音 / 辅助发音

An articulatory feature of a sound additional to its primary articulation. For example, a **dark 'l'** has the primary articulation of an **alveolar lateral**, and a secondary articulation of **velarization**.

Semi-vowel 半元音

Another term for **approximant**.

Sibilant 咝音 / 咝音性

A group of sounds, of the 's' variety, that generate a large amount of acoustic noise, including /s z ʃ ʒ/.

Sonorant 响音

A class of speech sounds that is produced without restriction to the airstream and can thus be sustained, e.g. **vowel**s, **nasal**s, **lateral**s. Contrast: **obstruent**.

Stop 塞音 / 闭塞音 / 爆破音

Another term for **plosive**, taking its name from the complete constriction that impedes the airflow, rather than the plosion of the release phase.

Stress 重读 / 重音

This refers, firstly, to the relative prominence of **syllable**s in the pronunciation of a word. In some languages stress is always on the same syllable, e.g. in Hungarian on the first syllable, in Polish generally on the penultimate syllable. In English, word stress is variable, e.g. in 'danger on the first syllable, in de'fence on the second. In words with multiple syllables, a secondary stress may occur in addition to the primary stress, e.g. on the final syllable in 'edu‚cate, or on the first syllable in ‚edu'cation. Word stress is sometimes called 'accent'. The second use of 'stress' is to refer to the syllables that receive prominence in the

intonation pattern of an utterance or part of an utterance (**tone unit**).

Stress-timed 重音节拍的   syllable-timed 音节节拍的

In a stress-timed language, such as English, the main stresses of words in connected speech fall at approximately equal intervals; whereas in a syllable-timed language, such as French, the syllables are approximately equidistant.

Suprasegmental 超音段（特征）

Features of pronunciation that accompany segments (**phonemes**), such as **stress** and **intonation**.

Syllabic consonant 音节（性）辅音

A consonant that functions as the nucleus of a **syllable**, which is normally a vowel. The word <u>button</u> /bʌtən/ in English is often pronounced /bʌtn̩/, where the /n̩/ is a syllabic consonant as the nucleus of the syllable /tn̩/. Similarly, the final /l/ in <u>giggle</u> may be syllabic: /gɪgl̩/.

Syllable 音节

Phonemes combine into syllables, and syllables combine into words. The 'nucleus' of a syllable is normally a vowel; it may have one or more consonants initially as 'onset', and one or more consonants finally as 'coda'. In English, up to three consonants may form an onset, e.g. <u>on</u> (none), <u>son</u> (one), <u>flop</u> (two), <u>strong</u> (three); and up to four consonants may form a coda, e.g. <u>to</u> (none), <u>top</u> (one), <u>tint</u> (two), <u>tilts</u> (three), <u>sixths</u> /sɪksθs/ (four). There are restrictions on the possible clusters of consonants in the onset and the coda, e.g. the first consonant of a three-consonant cluster as onset must be /s/: specifying the possibilities is the province of **phonotactics**. The structure of the syllable in English could be expressed as: (C) (C) (C) V (C) (C) (C) (C). Other languages have much more restricted potential for consonant clustering; in Korean, for example, a syllable may begin or end with a maximum of one consonant.

Tone language 声调语言

A language in which changes of pitch on a word may signal a change of meaning. The most well-known tone language is Chinese, but many languages of sub-Saharan Africa, of South America, and of East Asia are also tonal. Within Europe, Lithuanian exhibits tonality, and there are vestiges of it in Swedish, Serbian and Croatian.

Tone unit 语调单位

An **intonation** pattern is divided into tone units, which serve to chunk the information in an utterance. A tone unit contains a **nucleus**, which is the stressed syllable of the most significant word in the tone unit and is marked by a moving pitch (fall, rise, fall-rise, rise-fall). The nucleus is preceded by a 'head', usually uttered with a level pitch; and it may be followed by a 'tail', which continues the direction of the nuclear pitch.

Transcription 注音 / 音标 / 标音

The representation in phonetic symbols, usually from the **IPA**, of the pronunciation of a word or utterance. Transcriptions vary in the amount of phonetic detail that they contain, which depends on the purpose for which the transcription is being made. A 'broad' transcription usually represents phonemes only, together with word or sentence **stress**; it is usually enclosed within slash brackets / /. A 'narrow' transcription will include varying degrees of phonetic detail, e.g. **allophon**ic variation; it is usually enclosed within square brackets [ ].

Uvula(r) 小舌（音）

The uvula is the extension of the soft palate that hangs down at the back of the mouth and is used for blocking off the nasal cavity. A uvular consonant is made with the back of the tongue in contact or near-contact with the uvula. Uvular consonants are found in Arabic, but not usually in English, though the /k/ of <u>car</u> comes close to being uvular.

Velar 软腭音 / 舌面后音

A consonant sound produced by the contact or near-contact of the back of the tongue with the soft palate (**velum**), e.g. /k g/ in English.

Velarization 软腭音化

A **secondary articulation** that involves drawing the back of the tongue towards the **velum**, while making the primary articulation elsewhere in the mouth, e.g. for a **dark 'l'**.

Velum 软腭

The technical word for the soft palate, the part of the roof of the mouth beyond the hard palate and ending in the **uvula**. It functions in the production of **velar** consonants.

Vocal cords 声带

More technically the 'vocal folds', are a pair of fleshy membranes in the **glottis** that function in the production of speech sounds. Brought together, they produce a **glottal** stop; slightly ajar, they vibrate to produce voicing for voiced sounds; fully open, they allow normal breathing and the production of unvoiced sounds. Their manipulation also produces whispering, creaky voice, etc. – see **phonation**.

Voiced 浊音的 / 带音的   unvoiced 清音的 / 不带音的

A speech sound is either voiced, made with the **vocal cords** vibrating, or unvoiced, made without vibration of the vocal cords. **Vowel** sounds are normally voiced, while **consonant**s often occur as an unvoiced and voiced pair, e.g /p b/, /f v/.

Vowel 元音

A **sonorant** speech sound that is made by a configuration of the mouth without constriction of the airstream. The quality of a vowel sound is determined by: (a) the height of the tongue, on a scale of 'close' to 'open', or 'high' to 'low'; (b) where in the mouth the sound is made, front, central or back; and (c) the **rounding** of the lips, whether rounded or unrounded/spread. For example, /i/ is a 'close front spread' vowel, /ɒ/is an 'openback rounded' vowel, /ə/ is a 'mid central spread' vowel. Vowels normally function as the nuclei of **syllables**. See also **cardinal vowels**.

Grammar: morphology and syntax

Grammar 语法

A sub-discipline of linguistics concerned mainly with the structure of words (**morphology**) and sentences (**syntax**). The term 'grammar' is used to refer to: (1) the system of rules by which the words and sentences in a language are structured; (2) a theory or model that seeks to account for (1), e.g. Valency Grammar; (3) the description of (1) contained in a Grammar, e.g. *A Comprehensive Grammar of the English Language* (Quirk *et al.* 1985). Popularly, 'grammar' is also taken to include spelling and punctuation, but these are more properly considered in the context of the writing system for a language. Some linguists extend the scope of grammar to encompass the structure of texts (text grammar); see the entries under Discourse and Text Analysis.

Morphology 词法 / 词态学 / 构词学

Literally 'study of forms': the analysis of words into their constituent meaningful parts (**morphemes**). Morphology has two main branches: **inflectional** morphology and **derivational** morphology. Inflectional morphology considers the realization of grammatical **categories** as parts of words, such as plural number (<u>night-s</u>) or past tense (<u>talk-ed</u>). Derivational morphology is concerned with processes of **word formation**, and the identification of parts of words used in the creation of new lexical items, such as -er to derive an agent noun from a verb (employ-er, read-er).

Syntax 句法

Literally 'arrange together': the central part of grammar, involving the analysis of sentences into their constituents, including **clauses**, **phrases** and **words**. Syntax considers both the form of sentence elements (e.g. noun phrase) and their function (e.g. **subject** of the clause), as well as the resources for expressing grammatical categories (e.g. number, case, tense).

Accompaniment 伴随格 / 随伴格

Also called 'comitative': a participant in an action who accompanies the **agent**, usually expressed in English by the preposition with, e.g. 'She visited the museum with her mother-in-law'.

Accusative 受格 / 宾格

A type of **case**, associated with nouns that function syntactically as direct **object**, e.g. den Zug 'the train' in the German sentence 'Er hat den Zug verpasst' 'He missed the train'.

Active 主动（语态）　　passive 被动（语态）

Terms in the category of voice (more details at **voice**); illustrated by the difference between 'The junta put her under house arrest' (active) and 'She was put under house arrest by the junta' (passive).

Adjectival clause 形容词性从句 / 定语从句

A type of **subordinate clause** that functions like an **adjective**, i.e. 'describes' a noun. Adjectival clauses include **relative clauses** ('the decision which the committee endorsed') and **non-finite clauses** ('the decision endorsed by the committee', 'the noises coming from the locked room').

Adjective 形容词

Member of a **word class** that 'describes' nouns, used, in English, either in attributive position (before the noun), e.g. <u>an attractive proposition</u>, or in predicative position after a verb like <u>be</u>, e.g. <u>the proposition was attractive</u>.

Adjunct 附加语

A type of **adverbial**; a functional **slot** in the structure of sentences, associated with circumstances of time, place, manner, reason, etc. It is usually filled by an **adverb** ('Please walk <u>slowly</u>'), a **prepositional** phrase ('He sliced the ball <u>into the rough</u>'), or an **adverbial clause** ('She was visiting her grandfather <u>because he had been quite ill</u>').

Adverb 副词

Member of a **word class** that contains a variety of types of word, e.g. manner adverbs (<u>quickly</u>, <u>carefully</u>), time adverbs (<u>often</u>, <u>soon</u>), place adverbs (<u>here</u>, <u>there</u>), conjunctive adverbs (<u>however</u>, <u>therefore</u>), adverb particles (<u>on</u>, <u>off</u>, <u>up</u>, <u>down</u>).

Adverbial 状语

Sometimes used in the sense of **adjunct**, but sometimes with a broader reference, to include **conjunct** and **subjunct**, as well as adjunct.

Adverbial clause 状语从句

A type of **subordinate clause** that functions as **adverbial** in sentences. It is usually introduced by a subordinating **conjunction**, e.g. <u>although</u>, <u>because</u>, <u>if</u>, <u>so that</u>, <u>when</u> ('We are repairing the fence <u>so that the animals won't escape</u>').

Affected 受影响的（宾语）　　effected 表结果的（宾语）

Types of syntactic **object**. An affected object refers to an existing entity that is 'affected' by the action of the verb, e.g. 'The visitor has broken <u>the</u>

priceless vase'. An effected object is brought into being by the action of the verb, e.g. 'Andrew has written <u>a new poem</u> for the occasion'.

Affix 词缀

A **morpheme** that is attached to a word (root or stem) to form a new word or to realize an **inflection**. If attached before the root/stem, it is a **prefix** (e.g. <u>re-take</u>); if attached after the root/stem, it is a **suffix** (e.g. <u>fair-ness</u>). It is a convention to write affixes with a hyphen on the side that they are attached (or **bound**): <u>re-</u>, <u>-ness</u>. A word without any affixes is a **root**; one that has been affixed but may yet be further affixed is called a **stem**. In some languages, 'infixes' occur, which are affixes that interrupt a root. The term **suprafix** is used for a feature of stress or tone that functions as a morpheme, e.g. the stress difference between <u>'export</u> (noun) and <u>ex'port</u> (verb).

Agent 施事

The participant who instigates an action, usually the syntactic **subject** in a clause in the **declarative** mood, e.g. '<u>The warehouse</u> has dispatched your order'. In a **passive** clause in English, the agent is put in a <u>by</u>-phrase, e.g. 'Your order has been dispatched <u>by the warehouse</u>'. Compare **patient**.

Agglutinating 黏着语

A type of language whose morphology is characterized by a one-to-one relation of form to meaning, i.e. each morpheme has a single meaning or function, and words are built up by adding one morpheme to another in a prescribed order. Turkish is an example of an agglutinating language, e.g. the word <u>evleriden</u> is made up of <u>ev-</u> 'house', <u>-ler</u> 'plural', <u>-i</u> 'possessive', <u>-den</u> ablative case (i.e. 'from'), so 'from their houses'. Compare **isolating**, **synthetic**.

Aktionsart 行为类型 / 体态

German for 'type of action'; it refers to the lexical **aspect** of a verb, in terms of duration, completion and the like. Typical Aktionsarten includes: activity (e.g. <u>play</u> in 'The children are playing'), achievement (e.g. <u>burst</u> in 'The balloon burst'), accomplishment (e.g. <u>sell</u> in 'He sold his bicycle'), state (e.g. <u>live</u> in 'They live in Manchester').

(Allo)morph 词素变体 / 语素变体 / 形位变体

The realization of a **morpheme** in sounds (pronunciation) or letters (writing). A morpheme is an abstract element, e.g. {DECIDE}, {PLURAL}— conventionally written in capitals between brace brackets. It is usually realized by a particular sound or series or sounds, and by a letter or series of letters. {DECIDE} is usually realized by the sound sequence /dɪsaɪd/ and the letter sequence 'decide'. However, if the suffix <u>-ion</u> is added, the pronunciation and spelling of {DECIDE} change: /dɪsɪʒ-ən/ 'decis-ion'. The morpheme {DECIDE} is, therefore, said to have two 'allomorphs' (literally 'different forms'). Similarly, the {PLURAL} morpheme has a number of allomorphs, in both pronunciation and spelling, e.g. /z/ in <u>apple-s</u>, /s/ in <u>apricot-s</u>, and /ɪz/ in <u>peach-es</u>.

Apposition 同位语

Two contiguous linguistic items with the same reference, usually two noun phrases, e.g. 'Mr Plod, the policeman'. A noun phrase and a <u>that</u>-clause may also be in apposition, e.g. in 'the proposal that inheritance tax should be abolished', <u>that inheritance tax should be abolished</u> is the proposal; the <u>that</u>-clause elaborates the noun phrase.

Aspect 体

A category associated with the verb, relating to the way in which an action, event or state is viewed in respect of its distribution in time. For example, a distinction may be drawn between viewing an action or event as in progress and viewing it as occurring at a point in time, often termed the 'progressive/non-progressive' or 'durative/non-durative' aspect; e.g. in English the distinction between 'The children were eating their breakfast' and 'The children ate their breakfast'. The 'progressive' in English is expressed grammatically by the construction 'be + present participle (-ing)'. In French, the 'imperfect' inflections on the verb perform a similar function in relation to past time: 'Les enfants mangeaient leurs petit-déjeuners'. An aspect may also be signalled lexically rather than grammatically (by other words rather than by inflections or constructions). For example, repeated occurrence (**iterative**s or 'habituals') in English may be signalled by repeatedly or several times ('He shouted repeatedly'), or it may be part of the meaning of the verb ('The bird fluttered its wings'). Aspect meanings extend to **causative** (compare eat and feed 'cause to eat'), **inchoative**, i.e. beginning ('She started to sneeze'), 'conclusive' ('They've finished eating'). The aspect of a situation may, thus, be expressed by a combination of verb inflection, form of the verb phrase, meaning of the verb, or other items – usually adverbials – in the sentence (e.g. 'They used to and spend their holiday in Cornwall every year').

Auxiliary verb 助动词

A verb used together with a main verb to form different **tenses**, **aspects**, etc. In English, a distinction is made between 'primary' auxiliaries (be, have, do) and 'modal' auxiliaries (may/might, can/could, shall/should, will/would, must, etc.). The modal auxiliaries are used to express various kinds of **modality**, e.g. 'The letter may come tomorrow' (possibility), 'You can go outside in a minute' (permission). The primary auxiliaries have a number of functions: be is used with a present **participle** to form **progressive aspect** ('They were chatting about their holiday') and with a past participle to form **passive voice** ('They were stopped by a police officer'); have is used with a past participle to form **perfective** aspect ('They have already cast their vote'); and do is a dummy auxiliary used to form questions and negatives ('<u>Did</u> you <u>go</u> to the theatre?' 'We <u>didn't</u> <u>go</u> to the theatre').

Beneficiary 受益者
A participant in an action who benefits from it, e.g. <u>my mother-in-law</u> in 'I am baking my mother-in-law a birthday cake', or <u>me</u> in 'Save me a seat'. Compare **recipient**.

Binomial 二项式
A fixed phrase consisting of two words joined by <u>and</u>, usually nouns (e.g. <u>bed and breakfast</u>, <u>kith and kin</u>), but may also be from other word classes, e.g. verbs (<u>aid and abet</u>), adverbs (<u>to and fro</u>), prepositions (<u>over and above</u>). Binomials are usually 'irreversible', i.e. the order of the words cannot be reversed; so that <u>kin and kith</u> is not possible. English also has a small number of 'trinomials', e.g. <u>hook, line and sinker</u>.

Blend 合成词 / 混成词
A **word formation** process in which two words are coalesced (blended) to form a new word, usually with the initial part of the first and the final part of the second, e.g. <u>smog</u> from <u>smoke</u> and <u>fog</u>, but variations on this typical case are also found, e.g. <u>alcopop</u> from <u>alcoholic</u> and <u>pop</u> (colloquial term for a carbonated fruit drink) or <u>biopic</u> from <u>biographical</u> and <u>picture</u>.

Bound 黏着（词素）　　free 自由（词素）
Used of **morphemes** to indicate whether they can occur independently as a word (free) or whether they must be attached to another morpheme (bound). In English, **root** morphemes are usually free (<u>sad</u>, <u>sane</u>), and **affix** morphemes are always bound (<u>-ness</u>, <u>re-</u>, <u>-ity</u>).

Calque 仿译 / 直译 / 借译
Also called 'loan translation'; a type of **loanword** that involves translating

a term from the language from which it is borrowed into the language into which it is being borrowed. For example, <u>marriage of convenience</u> in English is a loan translation of French <u>mariage de convenance</u>, <u>world view</u> is a translation of German <u>Weltanschauung</u>.

Case 格

A grammatical **category** associated with nouns and pronouns; it reflects the syntactic **function** (subject, object, etc.) that a noun/pronoun has in a **clause**. The 'nominative' case is associated with **subject** function, the 'accusative' case with direct **object**, the 'dative' case with indirect object, and the 'genitive' case with possession. In Latin, case distinctions are realized in the inflectional suffixes of nouns; in German, they are reflected in the form of the article accompanying the noun [<u>der Baum</u> 'tree' (nominative), <u>den Baum</u> (accusative), <u>dem Baum</u> (dative), <u>des Baumes</u> (genitive)]. The term 'case' has also been used to refer to the semantic function of a noun/pronoun, e.g. in Case Grammar (Fillmore 1987); in this use of 'case' the terms include 'actor', 'recipient', 'affected', which relate to generalized semantic functions of clause elements.

Category 范畴 / 类型

A feature associated with a grammatical **class** of items. For example, the category of **number** is associated with the class of nouns. The category of number usually consists of the terms 'singular' and 'plural', of which the singular is usually 'unmarked' and the plural is **marked**, e.g. by an inflection (<u>box-es</u>). Also associated with the class of nouns in some languages is the category of **gender**, e.g. 'masculine' and 'feminine' in French, and additionally 'neuter' in German. In English gender is associated with pronouns (<u>he</u>, <u>she</u>, <u>it</u>), to which the categories of number and person (1st, 2nd, 3rd) are also applicable; e.g. <u>we</u> is a '1st person plural' pronoun. One further category typically associated with nouns and pronouns is **case**, with terms such as 'nominative' and 'accusative'. For English nouns, a case distinction is made between 'common' case (sister) and 'genitive' or 'possessive' case (sister's). Categories associated with the verb class include **tense** (present, past), **aspect** (progressive, punctual), **voice** (active, passive), **mood** (indicative, subjunctive).

Catenative 链接动词

From Latin catena 'chain'; a verb that is normally followed by another verb, in a kind of chain. For example, in English, try is usually followed by an **infinitive** (try to open the door), avoid is often followed by a present **participle** (avoid visiting the dentist).

Causative 使役（动词）

Making something happen. Some verbs are inherently causative, e.g. force in 'The police forced the door open'. Some verbs may be causative in some contexts; compare 'The children walked to the park' and 'The teacher walked the children to the park'. A non-causative verb may have a causative counterpart, e.g. eat and feed. In some languages, a causative affix may derive a causative verb from a non-causative one.

Class 类

Items grouped together on the basis of (a set of) common features. The most obvious grammatical classification is that of words into **word class**es. Most grammatical statements, though, relate to classes of items, rather than to individual ones. **Phrase**s are classified according to their structure and functions into 'noun phrase', 'verb phrase', etc. Similarly, **clause**s are classified into 'main' and 'subordinate', and then into 'nominal', 'adjectival', etc.; **sentence**s into 'simple', 'compound' and 'complex'; and so on.

Clause 小句／从句

The basic structure of **syntax**, comprising as a minimum a **predicator** ('Stop!'). Clauses may contain additionally a **subject** ('The old man smiled'), a **complement** ('The old man seems friendly'), a direct **object**

('The old man removed <u>his glasses</u>'), an indirect object ('The old man handed <u>his companion</u> his glasses'), and **adverbial**s ('The old man was sitting <u>on that bench yesterday</u>'). Clauses **function** primarily as **constituent**s of **sentence**s, but they may also function as constituents of other clauses ('They said <u>that the old man seemed friendly</u>' – object), or as constituents of **phrase**s ('the old man, <u>who seemed very friendly</u>' – relative clause). A distinction is made between **main clause**s and **subordinate clause**s: a main clause is normally **finite** and is equivalent to a **simple sentence**; a subordinate clause may be finite or non-finite and usually functions within other clauses or phrases (when it is sometimes called an 'embedded clause'), or as a subordinate constitutent to a main clause within a sentence ('The old man removed his glasses, <u>so that he could scratch his eyebrow</u>').

Cleft 分裂句 / 强调句型

A construction in which a sentence is split (cleft), usually in order to put emphasis or focus on one element. The cleft construction in English has the following form: '<u>It be</u> NP relative clause', e.g. 'It was Lydia who found the missing pieces' or 'It was the missing pieces that Lydia found'.

Clitic 附着词素

A **morpheme** that has the characteristics of an independent word (free form) but is normally **bound** phonologically to another morpheme. The possessive <u>'s</u> in English may be regarded as a clitic, since it attaches to the last word of a noun phrase and not necessarily to the possessor noun, e.g. <u>the man standing by the door's coat</u>. A clitic joined to the end of a word is called an 'enclitic', one joined to the beginning of a word is called a 'proclitic', e.g. the indefinite article in <u>an apple</u>, pronounced as /əˈnæpəl/.

Combining form 组合词素

A **morpheme**, originally from Greek or Latin, used in the formation of **neo-classical compound**s, e.g. <u>astro + naut</u>, <u>paed + iatric</u>. These forms are usually roots in Greek and Latin. Combining forms may also join with other elements to form hybrid compounds, e.g. astro + chemist. A few combining forms have become roots in English, e.g. mania, which is a combining form in klepto + mania.

Comment clause 评述小句

Used to refer to items like I think in sentences such as 'There is, I think, another point of view to consider', as well as to kinds of relative clause that comment on the whole of the preceding clause, e.g. 'She is going to visit her sister, which will be very good for her'.

Complement 补语

This term is used in at least two ways. It is sometimes used to refer to any element of a clause other than the **subject**, including elements that are also termed **object** and **adverbial**. Alternatively, its use is restricted to a particular element, viz subject complement (e.g. tired in 'The ramblers were tired') or object complement (e.g. outrageous in 'I consider your suggestion outrageous').

Complementation 补语成分

The (usually obligatory) elements that accompany a verb in addition to the syntactic **subject**, i.e. any **object**s, **complement**, or obligatory **adjunct**.

Complex sentence 复杂句

A sentence composed of a **main clause** and at least one **subordinate clause**. Compare **simple sentence**, **compound sentence**.

Compound 复合词

A word formed by the combination of two or more **root** morphemes, e.g. speedboat, speed bump, speed-read. As illustrated, they may be written solid, open or hyphenated. Most compounds are **endocentric** (a speed bump is a kind of <u>bump</u>), but some are **exocentric** (e.g. <u>butterfingers</u> is not a kind of 'fingers', <u>red tape</u> is not a kind of 'tape').

Compound sentence 复合句

A sentence composed of at least two **main clause**s in a relation of **co-ordination**. Compare **simple sentence, complex sentence**.

Concessive 让步从句

A type of **adverbial** clause, usually introduced by <u>(al)though</u> in English, which is used to 'concede' something, e.g. '<u>Although it is not highly recommended</u>, this restaurant serves some excellent food'.

Concord 一致

The 'agreement' in respect of a grammatical **category**, e.g. **number**, between two syntactic elements, e.g. subject and verb, adjective and noun. For example, there is concord of number between demonstrative <u>these</u> and noun <u>books</u> in the noun phrase <u>these books</u>: both are marked for plural; compare <u>this book</u> (singular). In <u>we were</u>, there is concord between subject pronoun (plural <u>we</u>) and verb (plural <u>were</u>); compare <u>I was</u> (singular). In the French noun phrase <u>les mains sales</u> (literally 'the hands dirty'), concord of plural number occurs between definite article <u>les</u>, noun <u>mains</u> and adjective <u>sales</u>; compare singular <u>la main sale</u>.

Conditional 条件从句

A type of **adverbial** clause, usually introduced by <u>if</u> in English (negatively by <u>unless</u>), which is used to set a condition in respect of the proposition in the **main clause**, e.g. '<u>If you call off the strike</u>, we can begin negotiations'.

Conjunct 连结性状语 / 联加语

A type of **adverbial**, which is used to signal an explicit relationship between sentences, usually by means of a conjunctive **adverb** such as however, therefore, nevertheless, etc.

Conjunction 连词

Member of a **word class** that is used to join clauses together, and sometimes phrases and words. A distinction is made between 'co-ordinating' conjunctions (and, but, or) and 'subordinating' conjunctions (because, if, since, while, etc.).

Constituent 构成成分

An element of a structure. The constituents of a **clause** might be a **subject** + **predicator** + **object** ('My wife + answered + the telephone'). The noun **phrase** the telephone has the constituents 'determiner + noun'. The constituents of the word telephone are the **combining form**s tele- + -phone. A 1940s American approach to syntactic analysis was called Immediate Constituent Analysis, represented by C. C. Fries's *The Structure of English* (1952).

Contraction 缩略 / 缩约

A reduced form of a **function word**, which then takes on a **clitic**-like feature, e.g. negative not in English with **auxiliary verb**s, as in can't, didn't, won't, or auxiliary is with **pronouns**, as in she's.

Conversion 词类转移 / 词性转换

The **word formation** process by which a new word is created without affixation simply by transferring the word to a new **word class**. For example, bottle noun becomes bottle verb [i.e. 'put into a bottle (noun)'], if conjunction becomes if noun in a big if. Recent examples include: doorstep (noun to verb), showcase (noun to verb).

Co-ordination （小句、短语或词的）并列

The joining of two **clauses** by means of a co-ordinating **conjunction** (in English, and, but, or) to create a 'compound sentence', e.g. 'Patrick went to the library, but Ruth worked at home'. Co-ordination may also occur between phrases (the boy and his horse), and between words (slow but sure).

Copula 系（动）词

A verb, in English usually be, which links a syntactic **subject** with its **complement** or an **adjunct**, e.g. 'The children are happy', 'They were in the garden'.

Coreference 同指关系

Having the same reference. For example, two noun phrases in **apposition** are in a relation of coreference (Menzies Campbell, the party leader), as are a noun phrase and a related pronoun ('Jenny Swift, I haven't seen her in years').

Countable 可数　　uncountable (mass) 不可数

The difference between nouns that can be counted and therefore have a plural form (idea, table) and those that cannot (bread, ink). If uncountables appear in the plural in English, it is usually with the meaning of 'kinds of', e.g. three French wines.

Dative 与格

A type of **case**, associated with nouns that function syntactically as indirect **object**, e.g. dem Kind 'to the child' in the German sentence 'Sie hat dem Kind ein Spielzeug geschenkt' 'She gave the child a toy'.

Declarative 陈述

The most common type of **mood**, associated with making statements, e.g. 'She arrived at the office late today'; traditionally called **indicative**.

Definite article 定冠词　　indefinite article 不定冠词

Members of the class of **determiner**, the and a/an, in English. The articles accompany nouns and indicate their status in ongoing discourse or text. The indefinite article marks a noun as new, or first mention; a definite article marks a noun as already mentioned, or identifiable from the linguistic or situational context. For example, in 'The train has arrived', the marks train either as already mentioned, or as the train we've been waiting for – the marks train as 'known to the hearer'.

Demonstrative 指示词

A member of the **determiner** class with **definite** reference, and additionally the notion of 'pointing'; represented in English by this/these and that/those, which differ in 'proximity', this being 'proximal' (to the speaker) and that being 'non-proximal', or 'distal'.

Deontic 义务（情态）

A type of **modality** concerned with obligation and permission, expressed in English by modal verbs such as should, ought to, must, have to; e.g. 'You should reply to the invitation as soon as possible'.

Derivation 派生词

A new word formed by the addition of an **affix** to a **stem**, e.g. re-state, friend-ly, coloniz-ation. Compare **inflection**.

Determiner 限定词

A small class of words that accompany nouns; the most common member is the definite article the (the reason). The class of determiners also includes: the indefinite article a/an (a field, an argument); the demonstratives this/that (this decision, those boxes); the possessives my, our, your, his, her, its, their (our address, her coat, its tail, their performance).

Deverbal 动词派生

Derived from a **verb**; so proposal is a deverbal noun, derived from the verb <u>propose</u>.

Dynamic 动态（动词）　　static 静态（动词）

Used of **verb**s to distinguish those whose meanings imply movement or change of state (dynamic) from those that do not (stative). In English, the distinction broadly correlates with those verbs that can have a **progressive** form (dynamic) and those that cannot (stative), e.g. 'I am learning Russian', but 'I know Russian' (not 'I am knowing').

Embedding 嵌入

The term used in some approaches to grammar to refer to **subordinate clause**s that have a function within another clause. For example, in 'They insist that the doors remain locked', the <u>that</u>-clause (<u>that the doors remain locked</u>) is embedded in the **main clause** (<u>They insist X</u>) as the syntactic **object**.

Endocentric 内中心 / 向心（结构）
exocentric 外中心 / 离心（结构）

In relation to a structure (**syntagm**), whether one of the elements can stand for the whole structure. In an endocentric structure, a 'head' is the minimal form; e.g. in an adjective **phrase**, the head is the adjective – compare <u>afraid</u>, <u>very afraid</u>, <u>very afraid to venture out</u>, in which the head is <u>afraid</u>. In an exocentric structure, at least two elements are obligatory, and neither can represent the whole structure, which therefore has no head; e.g. **subject** + **predicator** is minimal in a **clause** in English (<u>my watch + has stopped</u>), and preposition + noun phrase in a prepositional phrase (<u>from</u> + <u>the beginning</u>).

Epistemic 认知 / 知识（情态）

A type of **modality** concerned with the speaker's assessment of the possibility or certainty of some state of affairs, expressed in English by means of modal verbs such as <u>may</u>, <u>might</u>, <u>could</u>, <u>must</u>, as well as adjectives like <u>possible</u>, <u>probable</u> or adverbs like <u>maybe</u>, <u>possibly</u>, <u>certainly</u>.

Equative 等同句 / 等价句

A clause in which the **subject** and **complement** have **coreference** and are in principle reversible, e.g. 'Margaret is the manager of the department' – 'The manager of the department is Margaret'.

Ergative 作格语言

A language in which the syntactic **subject** of an in**transitive** verb is treated the same (e.g. by sharing the same **case** marking) as the **object** of a transitive verb, by contrast with the **agent** of transitive verbs. In 'accusative' languages, such as those of Europe, the subjects of both transitive and intransitive verbs are treated the same (e.g. by being marked as **nominative** case) and the object of transitive verbs is distinct (**accusative** case).

Existential sentence 存在句

A sentence that posits the existence of some entity, typically introduced by <u>there</u> in English, e.g. 'There is someone at the door', 'There are other matters to discuss'.

Experiencer 感受者

The term used to describe the syntactic **subject** of a **private state** verb, such as <u>believe</u>, <u>feel</u>, <u>like</u>, <u>suppose</u>. For example, in 'Everyone felt the earth tremor', <u>everyone</u> functions as experiencer.

Exponence 阶实现 / 阶标示 / 说明阶

Also sometimes called 'realization'; the relation between a semantic unit (proposition, concept) and its lexical and syntactic form; and in turn between a syntactic unit (word, sentence) and its expression in speech or writing (i.e. phonological and graphological form).

Extraposition 外位 / 外置

The syntactic process by which a clause functioning as the syntactic **subject** or **object** is put to the end of a sentence, and its place, in English, is taken by a dummy <u>it</u> pronoun. For example, in 'It was very difficult to convince the judge of his innocence', the subject infinitive clause (<u>to convince the judge of his innocence</u>) has been extraposed, and its usual, initial position is filled by <u>it</u>.

Factive 叙实（动词）

A factive verb commits to the truth of its **complementation**. For example, in 'I know that Jack is innocent', <u>Jack is innocent</u> is taken as fact – <u>know</u> is a factive verb. Substitute <u>assume</u> for <u>know</u>, and <u>Jack is innocent</u> is no longer taken as fact – <u>assume</u> is a non-factive verb.

Finite 限定（动词）　　non-finite 非限定（动词）

This distinction is applied to forms of **verbs**, verb phrases, and **clauses**. The finite forms of verbs in English are: present **tense** (<u>talk</u>, <u>talks</u>) and past tense (<u>talked</u>). The non-finite forms are: **infinitive** (<u>to talk</u>), present **participle** (<u>talking</u>), past participle (<u>talked</u>). The past participle normally has the same form as the past tense (<u>talked</u>), though not always (<u>showed/shown</u>, <u>sang/sung</u>). A non-finite verb phrase begins with a non-finite verb form (<u>seen</u>, <u>having decided</u>). A non-finite clause is one containing a non-finite verb phrase as the predicator (<u>to fetch a pail of water</u>, <u>sitting on the fence</u>, <u>smashed by the impact</u>).

Function 功能

The **constituent** of a structure is of a particular 'form' and has a specific 'function' in the structure. For example, <u>my wife</u> is a noun phrase (its form) and functions as **subject** in the **clause** 'My wife answered the telephone'. Other functions of clause constituents are: **predicator**, **object**, **complement**, **adverbial**. These, together with subject, are the functional slots of clause structure. Smilarly, words have functions in the structure of phrases, and morphemes in the structure of words. The term 'function' is also used to indicate the communicative purpose of a sentence; e.g. the **interrogative** 'Would you, please, sign here?' functions as a polite command. Some approaches to the description of language take a self-consciously functional approach, e.g. Givón (1993), Halliday & Matthiessen (2004).

Function word 虚词 / 功能词
content word 实词 / 实义词

Also called 'grammatical/lexical word'; a distinction between **word class**es that are open and with a large membership (content), which carry the main referential meaning of a sentence (noun, verb, adjective, adverb), and word classes that are closed and restricted in membership, and whose words carry grammatical meaning and serve to bind the content words together. Function words include members of the **determiner**, **pronoun**, **preposition** and **conjunction** classes, as well as **auxiliary verb**s, **conjunct**ive adverbs, and the like.

Future perfect 将来完成时

A tense which refers to a point in the future that looks backwards, expressed in English by shall/will have + past participle, e.g. 'In 2057 Ghana will have been independent for a century'.

Future tense 将来时

A tense that refers to future events and states of affairs. In French the future is formed by adding the present tense forms of avoir 'have' to the infinitive, e.g. je parlerai 'I will talk'. English has no equivalent form, but has a number of ways of referring to future time, including shall/will, be going to (I'll see you tomorrow, I'm going to wash the car).

Gender 性

A grammatical category associated with nouns and pronouns. In

European languages, the terms are 'masculine', 'feminine' and sometimes 'neuter'; approximating to real-world distinctions between 'male', 'female' and 'inanimate'. In English, the category is relevant only to the 3rd person singular pronouns (he, she, it). In French, nouns are classified into 'masculine' and 'feminine', indicated by the form of the determiner that accompanies them: le/un for 'masculine', la/une for feminine (le lapin, une reine). In German, it is the determiner accompanying a noun that is the principal indicator of gender, e.g. der Bleistift (masculine), die Tante (feminine), das Tier (neuter).

Genitive 所有格

A type of **case**, associated with possession and usually marking the possessor, e.g. in English 's (the child's toy), in German -(e)s (Gottes Haus 'God's house').

Goal 目标

The end point or destination of an action, compare 'source' and 'path'; e.g. 'They walked from the suburb (source) alongside the canal (path) to the city centre (goal)'. The term 'goal' has also been used to describe the syntactic **object** (as an alternative term for **affected**).

Head marking 中心语标记
dependent marking 依从语标记

In the structure of **phrases** and **clauses**, whether grammatical relations (e.g. **case**) are marked on the head of the phrase/clause or on the dependent(s). In English, the possessor (dependent) is marked and the thing possessed (head) is not, e.g. John-'s house; whereas in Hungarian, the reverse applies (head marking), e.g. Janos haz-á.

Hypotaxis 形合关系 / 主从关系

From Greek 'arrangement under'; this refers to the syntactic relation of subordination, especially in relation to clauses. A hypotactic style is one that uses a lot of **subordinate clause**s, often leading to a fairly dense syntax, which can be difficult for a reader/hearer to process. Contrast **parataxis**.

Imperative 祈使语气
The type of **mood** associated with the issuing of commands and usually realized in English by a sentence without a subject and with the base form of the verb, e.g. <u>Get out!</u> <u>Close the door</u>!

Imperfect 未完成式 / 不完全态
See **past tense, perfect(ive)**.

Inchoative 表始动词 / 起始动词 / 表始体
An inchoative verb or **aspect** refers to the beginning or onset of an action. In English, the verb <u>begin</u> could be regarded as an inchoative, as in 'The ice began to melt'; and <u>be about to</u> expresses inchoative aspect, as in 'They are about to take the vote'.

Indicative 陈述语气 / 直陈语气
The **mood** associated with the making of statements and usually regarded as basic by contrast with **imperative** and **subjunctive**. Compare **declarative**.

Infinitive 不定式
A form of the verb preceded in English by the infinitive marker *to*. e.g. <u>to come</u>, <u>to play</u>, <u>to snore</u>. A version of the infinitive sometimes occurs without <u>to</u>, e.g. after verbs of perception ('I heard you <u>snore</u>'). In other languages, the infinitive is marked by a suffix, e.g. <u>-er</u> in French <u>parler</u> 'to talk', <u>-en</u> in German <u>sehen</u> 'to see'.

Inflection 屈折变化 / 构形变化
The realization of a grammatical **category**, either by the addition of an

affix or by some change in a word **stem**. For example, the 'plural number' inflection in English is usually realized by the addition of the suffix -(e)s (star-s, church-es); alternatively by an alteration to the stem (foot – feet, louse – lice). Similarly, the 'past tense' inflection is normally realized by the addition of the suffix -(e)d (bake-d, look-ed), but also by a variety of alterations and or additions to the root (sang, slept, taught). Compare **derivation**.

Instrument(al) 工具

The entity that is used in order to carry out an action, often introduced by with in English, e.g. 'They analysed the data with a computer'.

Intensifier 强度副词 / 强调副词

A type of **adverb** that modifies adjectives and other adverbs, to give a more intense, emphatic meaning, e.g. very good, absolutely wonderful, completely sane.

Interrogative 疑问语气

The type of **mood** associated with asking questions or making requests. Two types of interrogative are recognized: 'yes/no' or 'polar', which expects either a 'yes' or a 'no' as an answer ('Is she in her office?'), and 'wh-' or content interrogatives, which are introduced by a **wh-word** and ask for some piece of information ('Where has she gone?' 'When will she be back?' 'Why isn't she there?').

Isolating 孤立（语）

Also called 'analytic'; a morphological type of language in which all words are free morphemes, and there are no affixes. Chinese, in all its varieties, is the most well-known isolating language. Compare **agglutinating**, **synthetic**.

Iterative 重复动词

Of a verb, repeating the action. For example, <u>bounce</u> in English is inherently iterative: 'Fred bounced the ball across the field' implies that the ball went between Fred's hand and the ground repeatedly. Iteration can be expressed in other ways, e.g. 'Fred was throwing the ball in the air' (the **progressive** form implies iteration), 'Fred kept on kicking the ball against the wall'.

Left-branching 左分支   right-branching 右分支

This refers to the tendency that languages have when ordering dependent elements in relation to a head. If the dependents come before the head, then it is called 'left-branching'; if after, then 'right-branching'. English has cases of both: in noun phrases, articles and adjectives precede the head noun (<u>a substantial,</u> <u>wholesome meal</u>); but in clauses objects follow verbs, and in sentences subordinate clauses tend to follow main clauses ('We'll see you tomorrow, <u>after</u> we've been shopping'). In Japanese by contrast, the left-branching tendency is more consistent: objects precede verbs, and adjectives precede nouns.

Lexeme 词位

The term for a **word** viewed lexically, e. g. as the headword of a dictionary entry. A lexeme may have a number of word forms, or **inflection**al variants, e.g. the lexeme <u>buy</u> has the forms <u>buy, buys, buying, bought</u>.

Loan translation 仿译 / 直译 / 借译

See **calque.**

Loanword 借词 / 外来词

A word that has been 'borrowed' from another language in order to fill a lexical gap in the borrowing language, e.g. <u>faux pas</u> from French into English. A large proportion of the English vocabulary is made up of loanwords, many of which have been adapted to the spelling and pronunciaton of English, e.g. bagel from Yiddish baygel, goulash from Hungarian gulyás, tsunami from Japanese.

Main clause 主句

Also called 'matrix clause'; the clause in a sentence that contains a **finite** verb phrase, and to which other clauses are subordinate, unless it is in a **compound sentence,** in which there may be two or more main clauses.

Marked 有标记的   unmarked 无标记的

In morphology, this refers to a grammatical **category**, one term of which may have no overt morphological marker. For example, in English, the singular **number** is unmarked, while the plural is normally marked (frog – frogs). The concept of 'markedness' has been extended to other areas of grammar and lexis, e.g. vixen is marked for 'female', as against unmarked fox, which is neutral as to 'male/female'.

Minor sentence 小句，不完全句

A structure deemed to be a clause or sentence but which does not contain a main verb, e.g. dinner over in 'Dinner over, they went into the garden'. Notices such as No Hawkers or Dogs on the loose are also considered to be minor sentences.

Modality 情态

An assessment by the speaker/writer of the degree of possibility or certainty associated with a statement (= **epistemic** modality), or an expression of the ability or necessity attributed to the subject of a sentence (= **deontic** modality). Modality is expressed in English by means of the modal **auxiliary verb**s, though not exclusively; e.g. 'possibility' may be expressed by may/might ('They may/might telephone this evening'), by possible or possibility ('It's possible they'll phone this evening'), or by perhaps or maybe ('Maybe they'll phone this evening'). 'Obligation' may be expressed by the modals must/should/

ought to ('You must/should visit your sick grandmother'), by be obliged ('You are not obliged to answer this question'), or by be necessary for ('It is necessary for you to undergo this test'). Modality is a complex area of grammar and much has been written on it from both a linguistic and a philosophical perspective; see Coates (1983), Palmer (1990).

Mood 语气

This refers to the distinction between 'declarative', 'interrogative' and 'imperative' types of **sentence**s. Declarative sentences, which are usually viewed as basic, function communicatively as 'statements'; their elements are normally ordered: **subject + predicator + object** etc. ('You + could get + a loaf of bread'). Interrogative sentences usually function communicatively as 'questions', and their structure involves subject-verb inversion ('Could you get a loaf of bread?'). Imperative sentences function as 'commands'; they have no subject and the verb is in its base form ('Get a loaf of bread!'). The 'subjunctive' mood survives only as a vestige in English ('If I were you …', 'God bless you!'), though it is found regularly in subordinate **conditional** and hypothetical clauses in some other European languages.

Morpheme 词素 / 形位 / 语素

A **constituent** of a **word**; it is meaningful and occurs with a constant meaning in the structure of other words; it is realized by a sequence of sounds in speech and of letters in writing; it may have more than one realization in either speech or writing (**allomorph**s). For example, the word immaturity is composed of the morphemes {IN-} {MATURE} {-ITY}; {IN-} is a negative prefix, which has the realization im- /ɪm/ before the initial 'm' of mature; the root {MATURE} loses final 'e' in spelling, since it is followed by a suffix beginning with a vowel; {-ITY} is a suffix that forms nouns from adjectives, as in equality, locality, vitality.

Morphophonemics 形态音位学 / 词素音位学

The analysis and description of the realization of **morpheme**s in speech (**allomorphs**), i.e. their **phonem**ic structure, especially where this is variable. Phonemic variation may be conditioned, e.g. the {PLURAL} morpheme in English is regularly realized by /s/, /z/ and /ɪz/. The /ɪz/ realization occurs where the final phoneme of the **stem** is a sibilant / s z ʃ ʒ tʃ dʒ/ (<u>roses</u>, <u>rushes</u>, <u>peaches</u>). Otherwise, the /s/ variant occurs after stem-final voiceless consonants (<u>lips</u>, <u>cuffs</u>, <u>sacks</u>), and the /z/ variant after stem-final voiced consonants and (voiced) vowels (<u>fads</u>, <u>bags</u>, <u>sums</u>, <u>boys</u>). The regular variants of the {PLURAL} morpheme are 'phonologically conditioned', i.e. determined by their phonemic environment, in this case the final sound of the stem to which the plural suffix is added. The (root) morpheme <u>either</u> may be pronounced /aɪðə/ or /iːðə/; nothing conditions the choice of realization, so they are 'in free variation'. The variation for the morpheme {CLEAR} between /klɪə/ and /klær/ is 'morphologically conditioned': /klær/ occurs when {CLEAR} is followed by a derivational suffix such as <u>-ify</u> or <u>-ity</u> (<u>clarify</u>, <u>clarity</u>), and /klɪə/ when {CLEAR} is not affixed or is suffixed by <u>-ness</u> (<u>clearness</u>).

Negation 否定

The expression of the denial or reverse of a state of affairs. In English, the most common negative expression is the **particle** <u>not</u>, which is positioned after the first auxiliary in a verb phrase and often contracts (<u>may not come</u>, <u>hasn't been seen</u>). Negation may, however, be expressed in a variety of ways ('No dogs allowed', 'You must never say that', 'She can be so uncaring').

Negative raising 否定提升 / 移前

The negative particle is moved (raised) from a subordinate clause into the main clause with verbs like <u>think</u>, but with no change of meaning, e.g. 'I think he won't come' becomes 'I don't think he'll come'.

Neo-classical compound 新古典复合词

A compound word formed from two **combining form**s, usually from either Latin or Greek, e.g. geo + phagy, xeno + phobia. A neo-classical compound is normally formed with an 'initial' combining form (ICF) and a 'final' combining form (FCF) from the same language; but a number of hybrid compounds have been formed, e.g. geo + stationary (Greek combining form + adjective originally borrowed into Late Middle English from Latin).

Nominalization 名词化 / 名物化

Changing a word from another **word class** into a **noun**, especially by **derivation**, e.g. cleverness (adjective to noun), supposition (verb to noun). A text full of nominalizations appears dense and impersonal.

Nominative 主格

A type of **case**, associated with nouns that function syntactically as **subject**, e.g. der Vogel 'the bird' in the German sentence 'Der Vogel sucht einen Wurm' 'The bird is looking for a worm'.

Non-finite clause 非限定性从句

A type of **subordinate clause** that contains a non-finite form of the verb phrase. The category of non-finite clause includes: **infinitive** clauses (to plant some birch trees), **present participle** clauses (planting some birch trees), **past participle** clauses (planted in the garden).

Noun 名词

Member of a large **word class** containing words that refer to people, things, ideas, etc. Nouns are often accompanied by a **determiner** (e.g. a/an, the) and sometimes by an **adjective** (a large forest).

Noun clause 名词性从句

A type of **subordinate clause** that functions in sentence structure where noun phrases usually occur, e.g. as **subject** or **object**; also called 'nominal clause'. The category of noun clause includes: <u>that</u> clauses ('She assumes <u>that the price will come down</u>'), <u>wh</u>-clauses ('Nobody knew <u>what they should say</u>'), **infinitive** clauses ('We would like <u>to view the house</u>'), **present participle** clauses ('I don't remember <u>seeing her at the party</u>').

Number 数

A grammatical **category** primarily associated with nouns and pronouns, but also with **determiners**. The terms are usually 'singular' and 'plural', although some languages have a 'dual' (for 'two'). In English, <u>window</u> is singular and <u>windows</u> is plural, <u>I</u> is singular and <u>we</u> plural, <u>this</u> is singular and <u>these</u> plural. The category of number is also relevant for verbs, where there is **concord** between subject and verb, e.g. <u>he/she/it walks</u>, where the <u>-s</u> inflection on the verb indicates '3rd person singular present tense'. In some other languages, such concord, involving 'person' and 'number', is more extensive, e.g. German: <u>ich laufe</u> (1st singular), <u>du läufst</u> (2nd singular), <u>er/sie/es läuft</u> (3rd singular). <u>wir/Sie/sie laufen</u> (plural).

Object 宾语

A syntactic **function** label for an element of **clause** structure; it occurs in addition to **subject** and **predicator** in **transitive** clauses; e.g. <u>her dinner</u> in 'Ruby has eaten her dinner'. A clause may contain a second object, in which case a distinction is made between 'direct object' and 'indirect object'. The indirect object usually represents the **recipient** or **beneficiary** of the action, e.g. <u>Ruby</u> in 'Mummy is giving Ruby her dinner'.

Paradigm(atic) 聚合

A 'vertical' relationship of substitution. In syntax, it refers to the items that can substitute for each other in a specific position within a pattern (**syntagm**). This can be expressed in general terms, e.g. in the pattern 'determiner + × + noun', position X may be filled by members of the class of adjectives. Or it may be expressed in specific, lexical terms, e.g. in the pattern 'the + × + fox', may be filled by <u>red</u>, <u>big</u>, <u>urban</u>, <u>lazy</u>, etc. In morphology, a paradigm is a model set of inflections for a class or subclass of words, e.g. in Old English an <u>a</u>-stem masculine noun is represented by the paradigm for <u>stān</u> (stone):

singular	nominative	<u>stān</u>	plural	nom	<u>stānas</u>
	accusative	<u>stān</u>		acc	<u>stānas</u>
	genitive	<u>stānes</u>		gen	<u>stāna</u>
	dative	<u>stāne</u>		dat	<u>stānum</u>

Parataxis 意合关系 / 并列关系

The arrangement of **clauses** in a relation of **co-ordination**, e.g. in **compound sentences.** Compare **hypotaxis.**

Participle 分词

A non-**finite** form of verbs. The **present participle** is formed by the addition of the <u>-ing</u> suffix in English (<u>driving</u>, <u>singing</u>, <u>walking</u>). The **past participle** is formed regularly by the addition of the <u>-ed</u> suffix (<u>decided</u>, <u>lifted</u>, <u>talked</u>), though there are many irregular formations (<u>bought</u>, <u>met</u>, <u>seen</u>). Participles are used in English together with **auxiliary verb**s to form **aspect**s, **tense**s and **voice**s. Many participles can also be used as adjectives, modifying nouns, e.g. <u>the singing detective</u>, <u>a bought loaf of bread.</u>

Particle 小品词

A short, invariable word with a grammatical function. In English, the adverb element of a phrasal verb is usually termed a particle, i.e. <u>in</u> in <u>give in</u>, or out in <u>turn out</u>. The **infinitive** marker <u>to</u> may also be called a particle, as in <u>to laugh</u>, <u>to sleep.</u>

Part of speech 词性 / 词类

An older, traditional term for **word class.**

Past participle 过去分词

A type of **participle,** whose regular form in English is the same as the past tense (<u>baked</u>, <u>frightened</u>), but compare <u>flew</u> – <u>flown</u>, <u>sang</u> – <u>sung</u>, <u>took</u> – <u>taken</u>. It may be the form of the verb in a **non-finite clause,** e.g. 'the child <u>given the prize</u>'. The past participle is used to form the **perfect(ive)** tenses (<u>has given</u>, <u>had sung</u>) and the passive **voice** (<u>is sung</u>, <u>was given</u>).

Past perfect 过去完成时

Also called 'pluperfect'; the **tense** that refers to events and states of affairs in the remote past, i.e. before the 'past'. The past perfect in English is formed with the past of the <u>have</u> auxiliary, followed by the past participle (<u>had reported</u>). The past perfect may be used for sequencing events in the past, the remoter event being in the past perfect, e.g. 'The newspaper <u>had reported</u> the proposal before the committee <u>considered</u> it'.

Past tense 过去时

Also called 'preterite'; the tense that generally refers to actions and events that took place and were finished in past time. In English, this form of the verb is sometimes called the 'simple past', because it is formed by adding the <u>-(e)d</u> suffix to the verb and not by using an auxiliary verb, e.g. 'The exhibition <u>opened</u> yesterday'. In some languages (e.g. French), the 'past' contrasts with the 'imperfect', which refers to an ongoing activity in the past, e.g. 'Ils <u>chantaient</u> dans l'église' ('They were singing in the church').

Patient 受事

A term used for the 'undergoer' of an action, also called **affected,** usually the syntactic **object** in a clause, e.g. <u>the cat</u> in 'Alice blamed the cat for the mess'. Compare **agent**.

Perfect(ive) 完成体

A type of **aspect**, formed in English with the **auxiliary verb** <u>have</u> followed by the **past participle** (<u>has fallen</u>, <u>had followed</u>). In English the (present) perfect(ive) usually indicates a state of affairs that began in the past but is continuing or is still relevant at the moment of speaking (They <u>have lived</u> here all their lives; I <u>have lost</u> my umbrella). In other languages a contrast is drawn with the 'imperfective', so that 'perfective' indicates an action or event viewed as complete or as a whole.

Periphrastic 兼语式（结构）/ 迂说式（结构）

The use of a phrase (in the sense of 'two or more words') to express a grammatical **category**, rather than, say, an **affix**. For example, the comparative and superlative forms of many (polysyllabic) adjectives in English are formed periphrastically with <u>more</u> and <u>most</u> rather than with the <u>-er</u> and <u>-est</u> suffixes: <u>more pleasant</u>, <u>most agreeable</u>.

Person 人称

A grammatical **category** associated with **pronouns** and verbs, usually with three terms: first person (<u>I</u>), referring to the speaker; second person (<u>you</u>), referring to the addressee; third person (<u>he</u>, <u>she</u>, <u>it</u>), referring to the people or things being talked about.

Phrase 短语

An element in the structure of a **clause**, fulfilling the roles of subject, verb, object, etc. In English, five types of phrase are recognized: noun phrase, verb phrase, adjective phrase, adverb phrase, and prepositional phrase. The first four types of phrase are **endocentric** structures, and the phrase is named after the 'head' word, which is the minimal form of the phrase, e.g. for the noun phrase, <u>computer</u>, <u>the computer</u>, <u>the latest computer</u>, <u>the latest computer advertised in the magazine</u>.

The prepositional phrase is an **exocentric** structure, requiring both a preposition and a noun phrase, e.g. <u>about</u> + <u>your computer</u>.

Pluperfect 过去完成时（同 past perfect）

See **past perfect**.

Portmanteau morph 并合语子

An/A **(allo)morph** that expresses terms of more than one grammatical **category**. For example, the <u>-s</u> suffix on English verbs (e.g. <u>sing-s</u>, <u>vote-s</u>) expresses 'third **person**', 'singular **number**', 'present **tense**'. The allomorphs of **inflectional** affixes in **synthetic** languages are regularly portmanteau, by contrast with those in **agglutinating** languages.

Possessive 所有（格）/ 所属（关系）

A relationship between a 'possessor' and a 'thing possessed', marked in English either by the <u>-'s</u> suffix on the possessor (<u>the president's duties</u>) or by an <u>of</u>-phrase containing the possessor (<u>the duties of the president</u>). Languages vary in how they express the possessive relationship; in some, possession is associated with **genitive** case.

Predicate 谓语 / 述语

In traditional grammar, the part of a sentence that is not the **subject**, e.g. in 'The police have arrested the suspects', <u>the police</u> is subject, and <u>have arrested the suspects</u> is predicate.

Predicator 谓词 / 谓语部分

The **functional slot** in **clause** structure that is filled by the verb **phrase**. For example, <u>has won</u> in 'Jason + has won + the race'. The predicator can be viewed as the pivotal element in a clause; the lexical verb influences the number and nature of the other clause elements; e.g. <u>win</u> expects a subject (usually human – the winner) and an object (the competition or game won). Valency Grammar starts from this assumption; see Allerton

(1982), Herbst *et al.* (2004).

Prefix 前缀

A type of **affix**, which is added to the front of a **stem** to form a new word, or in some languages, as an **inflection,** e.g. <u>pre-owned</u>, <u>sub-let</u>, <u>un-caring</u>.

Preposition （前置）介词   postposition 后置介词

Member of a **word class** that is used to connect a noun (phrase) to other elements in a sentence. Some languages, such as English, have prepositions (<u>at</u>, <u>from</u>, <u>into</u>, <u>of</u>, etc.), which come before the noun (phrase); others, e.g. Panjabi, have postpositions, which come afterwards.

Present participle 现在分词

A type of **participle**, formed in English with the <u>-ing</u> suffix (<u>buying</u>, <u>filling</u>, <u>spending</u>, <u>wishing</u>). It is used to form a type of **non-finite clause**. The **progressive** verb forms are composed of the **auxiliary verb** <u>be</u> followed by the present participle (<u>is buying</u>, <u>was spending</u>).

Preterite 过去时（同 past tense）

See **past tense**.

Private state 个体认知状态 / 主观认知状态

This refers to a group of verbs that express states of mind and emotion, known as 'private states', e.g. <u>believe</u>, <u>hate</u>, <u>like</u>, <u>wish</u>, <u>be angry</u>, <u>be excited</u>.

Progressive 进行体

A type of **aspect**, expressed in English by <u>be</u> + **present participle** (<u>is laughing</u>, <u>was crying</u>). It is sometimes called the 'continuous' or 'durative' aspect. The general meaning of the progressive is 'action or event happening at the time of speaking', i.e. in progress.

Pronoun 代词

A **word class** of **function** words that are used to substitute for **noun**s or noun phrases in ongoing discourse. The class includes, in English: personal pronouns (<u>I</u>, <u>she</u>, <u>you</u>, <u>we</u>, <u>they</u>), possessive pronouns (<u>mine</u>, <u>hers</u>, <u>theirs</u>), **reflexive** pronouns (<u>myself</u>, <u>himself</u>, <u>ourselves</u>), **demonstrative** pronouns (<u>this</u>, <u>that</u>), **interrogative** pronouns (<u>who</u>, <u>what</u>), **relative** pronouns (<u>who</u>, <u>whom</u>, <u>whose</u>, <u>which</u>), indefinite pronouns (<u>someone</u>, <u>anything</u>).

Quantifier 数量词

A class of words, sometimes regarded as a subclass of **determiner**s, which includes the numerals (cardinal – <u>two</u>, <u>eight</u>, <u>sixty</u>; ordinal – <u>second</u>, <u>eighth</u>, <u>sixtieth</u>) and the indefinite quantifiers, such as <u>many</u>, <u>several</u>, <u>some</u>, <u>a few</u>, <u>a lot of</u>. They are typically used with nouns to indicate specific numbers or some amount, e.g. <u>eight students</u>, <u>a lot of discussion</u>.

Recipient 与事／接收者

The semantic role of the person in an action who receives something from the **agent**, often expressed syntactically as an indirect **object**, and associated with **dative** case. In English, the recipient may be in a prepositional phrase introduced by <u>to</u>; compare 'Helen sent <u>her mother</u> a bunch of flowers', 'Helen sent a bunch of flowers <u>to her mother</u>'.

Reciprocal 相互（行为）

An action in which two participants engage mutually. Some verbs are inherently reciprocal, e.g. <u>kiss</u> in 'They are kissing'. Otherwise, in English, the reciprocal relation is usually expressed by <u>each other</u> or <u>one another</u>, e.g. 'They are hugging each other'. Compare **reflexive**.

Reduplication 重叠（法／式）

A **word formation** process in which part or all of a word is repeated, e.g.

wishy-washy, fuddy-duddy, nitty-gritty. In some languages, reduplication can also function as an **inflectional** process; in Latin, for example, the **preterite** of some verbs is formed by partial reduplication (of the first syllable), e.g. spondeo 'I vow' (present) – spospondi 'I vowed' (preterite).

Reflexive 反身

An action that someone performs on him/herself. Some verbs are inherently reflexive, e.g. shave in 'He is shaving'. Otherwise, in English, the reflexive relation is usually expressed by a 'reflexive **pronoun**' (herself, yourself, themselves, etc.): 'She has hurt herself'. In English and other languages, reflexive pronouns may also be used for emphasis, as in 'She finished the puzzle herself'.

Relative clause 关系从句

A **subordinate clause** with an adjectival function. In English, a relative clause is usually introduced by a relative pronoun (who, whom, whose, which, that) and follows the noun to which it relates (its antecedent), e.g. 'the tourists who visit Stratford'. A distinction is made between 'defining' and 'non-defining' (or 'restrictive' and 'non-restrictive') relative clauses. A defining relative clause serves to identify the noun being talked about, e.g. in 'my sister who married a Frenchman', the relative clause identifies which of my sisters I am referring to. On the other hand, 'my sister, who lives in Scotland' implies that I have only one sister, so that the relative clause is non-defining and merely adds additonal information about my sister. As is evident from these examples, in writing, a non-defining relative clause is preceded by a comma; and it is also normally terminated by a comma; whereas a defining relative clause has no commas surrounding it.

Root 词根

A type of **morpheme**, one which forms the kernel of a **word**, and to which **affix**es may be joined to form derivations. Most roots in English are free and so function as independent words; compare <u>compose</u> – <u>decompose</u> – <u>decomposition</u>, <u>right</u> – <u>righteous</u> – <u>righteousness</u>. A small number of roots are bound, e.g. <u>-couth</u> in <u>uncouth</u>, whereas in highly inflecting languages (Latin, Russian) bound roots for nouns and verbs are normal. A **compound** word is composed of more than one root, e.g. <u>fieldmouse</u>, <u>light bulb</u>, <u>skateboard</u>. Once a root has been affixed, it becomes a **stem**.

Semelfactive 瞬间动作 / 一次性事件

An **Aktionsart** expressing a momentary (or punctual) action, e.g. of verbs in English, such as <u>burst</u> ('The balloon burst'), <u>sneeze</u> ('The detective sneezed'), <u>shatter</u> ('The glass shattered'). If the meaning becomes repetitive (**iterative**), then the verb is no longer semelfactive.

Sentence 句子

A syntactic structure (**syntagm**) composed of one or more **clauses**. Normally one of the clauses must be a 'main clause', with a **finite** verb phrase as **predicator**. Otherwise, the sentence is said to be a **minor sentence**, e.g. 'Nothing new to report'. If two main clauses are joined by a co-ordinating conjunction (<u>and</u>, <u>but</u>, <u>or</u>), it is said to be a **compound sentence** ('Harry became a soldier, and William went into the church'). If a **subordinate clause** is joined to a main clause, it is said to be a **complex sentence** ('You must arrange the pieces, so that you make a square'). Arguably, sentences are a construct of writing; they are not easily identifiable in speech (Carter & McCarthy 1997). The terms 'sentence' and 'clause' are used variously in different models of grammar.

Simple sentence 简单句

A sentence composed of a single **main clause**. Compare **compound sentence**, **complex sentence**.

Slot 空位　　filler 填充成分

The view of the structure of **clause**s that identifies a number of slots corresponding to syntactic functions such as **subject, object, complement, adjunct**, each of which may be filled by a number of types of phrase or clause. For example, in English, the complement slot may be filled by an adjective phrase ('That girl is <u>very pretty</u>'), a noun phrase ('His sister is <u>an accountant</u>'), an infinitive clause ('The proposal is <u>to increase the tax on tobacco</u>'), etc.

Stem 词干

A **word (root + affix)** that may be further affixed to derive a new word, e.g. <u>sensible</u> is a stem (composed of root <u>sense</u> + suffix <u>-ible</u>) that can be further affixed by <u>-ity</u>, to form <u>sensibility</u>.

Subject 主语

A **functional slot** in **clause** structure, usually filled by a noun phrase, representing the 'doer' (**agent**) of an action ('<u>This architect</u> designed the bridge'), the 'undergoer' of an event ('<u>The climber</u> slipped on the loose stones'), and the **experiencer** of a thought or emotion ('<u>Our children</u> enjoyed the holiday'). The subject is normally the initial element in an English clause, preceding the **predicator**; however, it inverts with an auxiliary verb to form an interrogative ('Has <u>this architect</u> designed many bridges?'). In English, a clause is normally composed of at least a subject + predicator.

Subjunct 次修饰语 / 次修品

A type of **adverbial** that is of a subordinate nature, expressing such notions as point of view ('<u>Economically</u>, the policy is not sustainable'), politeness ('Would you <u>kindly</u> open the door?'), emphasis ('<u>In fact</u>, nothing like that ever happened').

Subjunctive 虚拟语态 / 虚拟语气

A mood that expresses a variety of meanings, especially in **subordinate clauses**, such as 'unreal' conditions (If I were you, …), commands and decisions ('The committee decided/ordered that the doctor be struck off'), wishes (Long live the king!). In English, the few uses of the subjunctive are mostly fossilized, as in if I were you, and the use for decisions/orders is more common in American usage than British, where the alternative with should is preferred (that the doctor should be struck off). In other languages (e.g. French, German), the subjunctive is in more common use.

Subordinate clause 从句 / 从属小句 / 从属子句

A clause that does not normally occur on its own, but either in combination with a **main clause** to form a complex **sentence** ('We are not going to buy a new car, because we cannot afford it') or as part of another clause, as an 'embedded' element ('The student protested that he had not intended to cheat' – that-clause is **object** of protest). Embedded subordinate clauses may function as **subject**, **object** or **complement** in another clause, or as a **relative clause**.

Suffix 后缀

A type of **affix** that is added to the end of a **stem**, either to form a new word (**derivation**) or as an **inflection**. The following are derivations in English: bear-able, arrange-ment, rapid-ity, slow-ness, solid-ify. The following are inflections: grass-es, seek-s, creat-ed, think-ing, soon-er, thick-est.

Suppletion 异干互补

A morphologically related form that has inherited no sounds or letters from its source. For example, went is related to go, i.e. it realizes 'go + past tense', but it is a suppletive form. Similarly, better is a suppletive form, equivalent to 'good + comparative'.

Suprafix (superfix) 上缀

Also called 'superfix'; a type of **affix**, usually of stress or tone, which accompanies a morpheme. For example, the derivation of the noun import /ˈɪmpɔːt/ from the verb import /ɪmˈpɔːt/ is by means of a suprafix of stress, shifted from the second to the first syllable.

Syntagm(atic) 组合

The chaining of elements together to form a structure (syntagm); contrasts with **paradigmatic**, the substitution (choice) relation between elements. It refers to the syntactic 'rules' that form structural patterns; e.g. that an adjective phrase may have the structure 'adverb + adjective + complement' (very fond of ice-cream), or that a neo-classical compound may have the structure 'initial combining form + final combining form (anthrop + ology, bi + opsy, helio + phyte).

Synthetic 综合型（语言）

Also called 'polysynthetic'; a morphological type of language, in which grammatical categories are usually expressed by means of inflectional affixes, which are normally realized by **portmanteau morph**s. Latin and Greek are good examples of synthetic languages. Compare **isolating**, **agglutinative**.

Tag question 反义疑问句／附加疑问句／尾加问句

An **interrogative** that is tagged on to a clause, seeking confirmation or otherwise the truth of the proposition, e.g. 'Audrey Hepburn starred in *My Fair Lady*, didn't she?', 'The cedar isn't a deciduous tree, is it?'.

Tense 时态

The grammatical **category** that relates to real-world time, with the terms 'present', 'past', 'future', etc. In English, only the past tense is marked by **inflection**, normally -ed (entailed, refused), and the 3rd person singular present tense (entails, refuses). Other tenses are formed by using auxiliary verbs (sometimes called 'compound tenses'), e.g. **pluperfect** or 'past-in-the-past' (had refused), **future perfect** or 'past-in-the-future' (will have refused). There is no necessary one-to-one correspondence between tense and time, e.g. the use of the present tense for past time story telling, especially in informal registers ('And this chap comes into the room …'). Tense intersects with **aspect** to express the location and distribution of an action or event in time, and the perspective from which it is viewed. Tense and aspect systems in languages show great complexity and subtlety of expression. See: Palmer (1988), Leech (1972).

Transitive 及物的

A term used of both **verbs** and **clause**s. A transitive verb is one that is normally followed by an **object** ('They have postponed the match'), while an intransitive verb is not ('The storm has passed'). Similarly, a transitive clause is one that contains a transitive verb and an object, and an intransitive clause contains no object. Transitive clauses can normally be made passive (see **voice**); the object of the active clause becomes the **subject** of the passive clause ('The match has been postponed'). Verbs are traditionally marked as transitive or intransitive in dictionaries, but this simple distinction does not do justice to the range of **complementation** patterns that occur in clauses. Transitivity is the term used by systemic-functional grammar to refer to the relationships between the elements of a clause (Halliday & Matthiessen 2004).

Verb 动词

A class of words that are used to form verb phrases. It has subclasses of **auxiliary verb** and lexical verb. Lexical verbs refer to the action, event or state that a **clause** is about; auxiliary verbs combine with a lexical verb to form **tenses**, **aspects**, **voices**, etc. The term 'verb' is also sometimes used as an alternative to '**predicator**', to refer to the functional **slot** in clause structure. Grammatical descriptions that use 'verb' for both purposes can be confusing, though in the predicator sense, 'Verb' is often spelled with an initial capital letter.

Voice 语态

A grammatical category with the terms 'active' and 'passive'. In English, a **transitive** active **clause** expressing an action has the elements in the order 'doer – action – undergoer' ('The barber shaved a client'). In the passive clause, the undergoer becomes **subject**, the verb is in the passive form (**auxiliary** <u>be</u> + past **participle**), and the doer may be included in a phrase introduced with <u>by</u> ['A client was shaved (by the barber)']. Some languages have a 'middle' voice in addition to active and passive, e.g. with some reflexive verbs in French (<u>elle se lève</u> 'she rises'). French uses the same verb (<u>lever</u>) for English 'raise' and 'rise'; in this case, English uses a different lexical verb for the French middle voice of <u>lever</u>. But compare English 'She opened the door' (active) – 'The door was opened' (passive) – 'The door opened' (middle?).

Wh-word （特殊）疑问词

A set of words in English, most of which begin with <u>wh</u> (<u>who</u>, <u>what</u>, <u>whether</u>, <u>when</u>, <u>where</u>, <u>why</u>; the exception is <u>how</u>) that are used mainly as **conjunctions** to introduce <u>wh</u>-clauses ('He didn't know <u>who was coming to the party</u>'; 'They were wondering <u>how to unlock the door</u>'), or as **interrogative** pronouns or adverbs ('<u>What</u> did you say?', '<u>Where</u> did you put my book?').

Word 词

In syntax, the elements that enter into the construction of **phrase**s; in writing, a sequence of letters bounded by spaces; in **morphology**, a unit composed of one or more **root** morphemes, which may be **affix**ed; in lexicology, the basic unit of study. A word in lexical terms (**lexeme**) may be composed of more than one written (orthographic) word, e.g. phrasal verbs such as <u>give up</u>, <u>take off</u>, open **compound**s such as <u>fire engine</u>, <u>salt cellar</u>.

Word class 词类

A set of words grouped on the basis of shared syntactic **functions**, shared **inflection**al and **derivation**al morphology, and to some extent shared reference. A distinction is made between 'open'/'lexical' word classes (noun, verb, adjective, adverb) and 'closed'/'grammatical' classes (pronoun, determiner, preposition, conjunction). The closed classes have a relatively small and stable membership, and their main function is to provide grammatical information and linkages in the structure of phrases, clauses and sentences. The open classes are both large and continually expanding, and their members bear most of the referential meaning of a structure. There is probably a scale from 'fully lexical' (most nouns and adjectives) to 'fully grammatical' (some determiners), but other classes situated more to one end than the other of the scale.

Word formation 构词法

The processes by which new **word**s are coined in a language, including: **compound**ing (<u>moon + light, anthropo- + -ology</u>), **derivation** (<u>re- + invent, care + -less + -ness</u>), **blend**ing [<u>mot</u>(or) + (hot)<u>el</u>, <u>bio</u>(graphical) + <u>pic</u>(ture)], backformation (<u>troubleshoot</u>, from <u>troubleshooter</u>), acronyms (<u>CD-ROM</u> 'compact disc, read only memory').

Word order 词序

Usually refers to the basic order of clause elements in a language. For example, in English, the order is Subject – Verb – Object (SVO); in Japanese and Korean, the basic word order is Subject – Object – Verb (SOV); one of the basic orders for Modern Greek is VSO. In some languages, like English, word order is relatively fixed, because it serves to identify which element functions as **subject** or **object**; whereas in Greek the order is relatively flexible, because subject and object are marked by **case** inflections.

Semantics and pragmatics

Semantics 语义学

The study of meaning. Semantics is also a branch of philosophy; but within linguistics it encompasses the meaning of words (lexical semantics) and the meaning of sentences. The meaning of texts and discourses is sometimes taken to be part of semantics, as well; but this is where semantics and pragmatics largely overlap.

Pragmatics 语用学

The study of language in context, in particular how context influences the interpretation of language. It looks at how we make sense of utterances in ongoing discourse, the kinds of inferences that we draw, and the rules that we observe in order to participate successfully in conversation. An important topic in pragmatics is 'politeness' (see website of Linguistic Politeness Research Group: www.lboro.ac.uk/departments/ea/politeness).

Ambiguity 歧义

Where two or more interpretations (meanings) are possible of a single expression. For example, 'I spoke to the girl in the garden' could mean either 'there was this girl and the place I spoke to her was the garden' or 'there were two girls, one in the house and one in the garden, and I spoke to the one in the garden'.

Antonymy 反义关系

The **sense relation** of oppositeness. Three types of antonymy are usually recognized. (1) Gradable antonymy: pairs of adjectives that are on a more/less scale, e g. wide/narrow, beautiful/ugly; the quality is relative to the object being described (wide/narrow of roads is different from that of ribbons). (2) Complementary antonymy: pairs of words that are in an either/or relation of oppositeness, e.g. true/false, win/lose. (3) Converse antonymy: pairs of words that express the converse of each other, e.g. husband/wife, buy/sell, before/after; if Celia is Richard's wife, then Richard is Celia's husband.

Argument 论元 / 主目

An entity associated with a **predicate**. For example, the predicate throw has three arguments: the 'actor' (i.e. the thrower), the 'patient' or 'undergoer' (the thing thrown), and the 'goal' (where it is thrown).

Collocation （习惯性）搭配

The regular co-occurrence of two words. Collocation may be 'grammatical', when it mainly refers to the assocation of a verb, adjective or noun with a given preposition, e.g. rely + on, afraid + of, fondness + for. Collocation proper is lexical and may be expressed statistically as a greater than chance likelihood that one word will occur in the context of another, e.g. kettle and boil, chance and sheer.

Componential analysis （语义）成分分析法

The theory that the meanings of words can be analysed into a finite number of reusable semantic components. For example, the meaning of vixen could be said to have the following components: [+ mammal] [+ adult] [−male] [+ vulpine].

Connotation 内涵

The emotive overtones that a word carries, over and above its **denotation**al meaning. For example, <u>mob</u> has connotations of 'unruly' and 'ill-intentioned' by comparison with <u>crowd</u>; and <u>champagne</u> may be said to connote celebration or high living.

Constative 表述语

A type of **speech act** that asserts or states that something is so, and which can be evaluated as true or false, e.g. 'The doctor called five minutes ago'. Compare **performative**.

Conversational maxim 会话准则

Introduced by the philosopher, Paul Grice, these are 'rules' for participating in conversation. Grice proposed four maxims: quality (be truthful), quantity (be as informative as is necessary), relevance (fit in with the developing interaction), and manner (be clear, orderly, and brief).

Co-operative principle （会话）合作原则

The principle shared by participants in a conversation, which enables the conversation to be successful. There is said to be an understood principle of co-operation that participants abide by; otherwise, conversations would be derailed and would not achieve anything.

Deixis 指示词／指示语

The system of linguistic features that points outside of a text to the situational context. The features include: personal pronouns, especially first and second person (<u>I</u>, <u>you</u>), which serve to identify speaker(s) and addressee(s); demonstratives (<u>this</u>, <u>that</u>), which imply 'pointing'; adverbs like <u>now/then</u>, <u>here/there</u>, which point to real-world time and space.

Denotation 外延

The relation between a word and what it refers to in the real world;

the basic, core meaning of a word, as given in a dictionary definition. Contrast **connotation**.

Entailment 蕴涵

The truth of one proposition follows from the truth of another. For example, 'The ex-president has been hanged' entails that 'The ex-president is dead'. Compare **presupposition**.

Face-threatening act 威胁面子的行为

In **politeness** theory, a linguistic act that threatens an interlocutor's 'face', which includes their self-esteem, social identity and public image. It could be an utterance that is perceived as insulting, or just a challenge to a person's public persona. Abbreviated as 'FTA'.

Felicity condition 适切条件

Conditions that need to be in place for a **speech act**, especially a **performative**, to be valid. Felicity conditions may include 'preparatory conditions' (e.g. that the person performing a marriage is authorized to do so) and 'sincerity conditions' (e. g. that the person is committed to what they say).

Generic reference 类指

Reference to a class of things, as against individuals. For example, tiger(s) in the following all have generic reference: 'Tigers are ferocious beasts', 'The tiger is a ferocious beast', 'A tiger is a ferocious beast'. In all cases, tigers in general are being referred to, not any individual tiger(s).

Hedge 模糊限制语

A word or phrase that lessens the speaker's commitment to what they are saying. This could be done by using adverbs such as perhaps or maybe; or by using expressions such as sort of or if you know what I mean; or by using a personal disclaimer such as in my view, as far as I'm concerned.

Homonymy 同音同形异义关系

Two words are homonyms if they share the same spelling and pronunciation but are unrelated in meaning or have a different etymology. For example, <u>ear</u> 'organ of hearing' and <u>ear</u> 'head of a cereal plant' are homonyms. So are <u>sound</u> 'noise', <u>sound</u> 'whole, healthy', <u>sound</u> 'measure the depth of', and <u>sound</u> 'narrow sea channel'. Homographs are words that are spelt the same but pronounced differently, e.g. <u>tear</u> (from crying) and <u>tear</u> (rip in a garment or cloth), <u>wind</u> (movement of air) and <u>wind</u> (to turn or coil). Homophones are words that are pronounced the same but spelt differently, e.g. <u>steal/steel</u>, <u>fare/fair</u>.

Honorific 敬语

A linguistic marker, e.g. a morpheme, clitic, term of address, that shows respect to the addressee. Some languages, e.g. Korean, Japanese, have elaborate systems of honorifics, which vary according to who is addressing whom.

Hyponymy 上下义关系

A **sense relation** where words are in a hierarchical, 'kind of' relation. A superordinate term (hypernym) may have a number of (co-)hyponyms, e.g. <u>flower</u> has hyponyms <u>daffodil</u>, <u>tulip</u>, <u>rose</u>, <u>violet</u>, etc. Each of these hyponyms may, in turn, be a hypernym of more specific terms (its co-hyponyms).

Idiom 习语 / 成语

A more-or-less fixed expression whose meaning is not the sum of its constituents and is usually non-literal, i.e. figurative or metaphorical. Sometimes, an expression may have both a literal and a figurative meaning, e.g. <u>spill the beans</u>, <u>let the cat out of the bag</u>. For other idioms, only a figurative meaning is possible, e.g. <u>a storm in a teacup</u>, <u>face the music</u>.

Implicature 隐涵 / 含意

Something that is stated obliquely rather than directly, so that the hearer has to draw the implication from what it said. For example, if on a country walk someone suddenly shouted <u>Bull!</u>, you would take this as advice to run as fast as possible for the nearest gate. Again, within a household, the statement <u>The phone's ringing</u> would usually be taken to mean, 'Would you answer the telephone?'

Mand 指令性（言语行为）

A type of speech act, the purpose of which is to persuade or force someone to do something, e.g. a command, request, instruction.

Meronymy 部分—整体关系

A **sense relation** where words are in a hierarchical 'part of' relation. For example, <u>foot</u> can be said to have the meronyms <u>heel</u>, <u>instep</u>, <u>toe</u>, <u>ball</u>, <u>sole</u>, etc.

Metaphor 隐喻

A meaning that is non-literal, figurative. When not used of a literal 'foot', the word <u>foot</u> has metaphorical meaning, e.g. when used of a 'mountain' or a 'bed', or when used in the sense of 'pay' (<u>foot the bill</u>). Sometimes, metaphors can be extended and applied to a quite different sphere from the literal one; for example, the vocabulary of warfare is used extensively in politics, where elections are <u>fought</u>, one has political <u>enemies</u>, one engages in a <u>campaign</u> for election or for a policy, a bill may be <u>defeated</u> in Parliament, and so on. See Lakoff & Johnson (2003).

Ostensive definition 实指定义 / 直指定义

Defining the meaning of a word by pointing, clearly only possible with tangible objects. Pictorial illustrations in dictionaries could be regarded as a type of ostensive definition.

Performative 行事话语

A type of **speech act**, the utterance of which performs the act, e.g. saying 'I pronounce you husband and wife' at a marriage ceremony, or 'I name this ship "The Ark"' at a ship-naming ceremony.

Politeness 礼貌

Theories of politeness have been developed in pragmatics to account for ways in which participants in conversation strive to 'maintain' their interlocutor's 'face'. Politeness might take the form of **hedging** ('Could you, possibly, sort of, would you really mind …'), indicating deference ('Excuse me, officer, could you, please, tell me the time?'), apologizing ('I'm terribly sorry to intrude, but …'). The classic text on politeness is Brown & Levinson (1987).

Polysemy 一词多义 / 多义词

Words that are polysemous have multiple meanings. The meanings (senses) of a word are usually distinguished according to the contexts in which the word is used. When dictionaries list multiple meanings for a word, this is based on the analysis of the contexts in which the word is found to occur; dictionaries do not always agree on where to draw the lines between a word's meanings. Polysemy should be distinguished from **homonymy**. A word's meanings may differ considerably (e.g. those for table), but if they are all associated with the same word etymologically, then it is a case of polysemy and not homonymy.

Predicate 谓语 / 述词

The nucleus of a proposition, usually a verb, sometimes an adjective. A predicate will have a number of **arguments** associated with it, e.g. the predicate propose normally has two arguments: actor (the proposer) and undergoer (the proposition); the predicate fond has two arguments: the 'experiencer' (who has feelings of fondness) and the 'goal' (the object of the fond feelings).

Presupposition 预设

A background belief or assumption behind a proposition. For example, 'The King of England is bald' presupposes that England is ruled by a king. Compare **entailment**.

Proposition 命题

A sentence or statement viewed from the perspective of its meaning. A proposition is composed of a **predicate** together with its associated **argument**s.

Prototype 原型

An approach to word meaning that regards semantic categories as fuzzy and suggests that for any word we have a notion of what is prototypical about its meaning, so that some instances will fall centrally into the category, while others will be more peripheral, perhaps shading off into another category. For example, a prototypical tree has a trunk, branches, twigs, and leaves; but there are cases where we might call something a tree, even though it doesn't have all the prototypical features, e.g. rose tree (as against rose bush).

Reference 所指 / 指称

The relation of meaning between a word or expression and the entity in the context to which it is intended to point. The same entity may be referred to by different words or expressions, e.g. Fred, my father, he. Compare **denotation**.

Sapir-Whorf hypothesis 萨皮尔—伍尔夫假说

The notion, associated with the names of American linguists Edward Sapir (1884–1939) and Benjamin Lee Whorf (1897–1941), that there is a relation between the grammatical and semantic categories of a language and the way its speakers see and experience the world. The strong version of the hypothesis is 'linguistic determinism': the categories inevitably determine how the world is seen. The weaker version is 'linguistic relativity': cultures vary in line with how languages talk about and classify experience.

Semantic field 语义场

The words associated with a specified area of meaning, also called 'lexical field'. For example, the verbs of communication (<u>say</u>, <u>speak</u>, <u>tell</u>, <u>propose</u>, <u>argue</u>, etc.) might constitute a semantic field. Semantic fields enable us to see how semantic space is divided up by the vocabulary of a language, as well as indicating the lexical resources available for expressing given meanings.

Semantic prosody 语义韵

The positive or negative connotation that pervades a sentence containing specific words. For example, <u>commit</u> has a negative semantic prosody, since the acts that can be committed are generally negative, e.g. <u>crime</u>, <u>fraud</u>, <u>suicide</u>, <u>blunder</u>, etc.

Sense relations 意义关系

The meaning relations that words contract with each other in the vocabulary, as opposed to meaning relations of **denotation** or **reference**. The class of sense relations includes: **synonymy, antonymy, hyponymy, meronymy**. The classic text is Cruse (1986).

Speech acts 言语行为

The idea, introduced by the philosopher J. L. Austin, that what we say is equivalent to an action. He noted in particular 'performatives', where the utterance effects what it says, e.g. when someone launching a ship utters the words 'I name this ship HMS Pinafore', then the ship is so named. Austin's theory was further developed by J. R. Searle, and a distinction was made between 'locution' (the utterance itself), 'illocution' (what the utterance is intended to achieve), and 'perlocution' (the effect on the hearer).

Synonymy 同义关系

The **sense relation** of sameness or similarity of meaning. Two words are said to be synonyms if their meanings overlap substantially in one or more of their senses, e.g. hide/conceal, propose/suggest, old/ancient, earth/soil.

Discourse and text analysis

Discourse 话语 / 语篇

This term is sometimes used to refer to both spoken and written structures above the level of the sentence; some linguists, though, use it to refer only to spoken structures, with **text** being used for written ones. Spoken discourse encompasses 'monologue' (produced by a single speaker), 'dialogue' (with two speakers), and 'multi-party conversation' (with three or more speakers). Spoken discourse may be 'scripted' (written to be spoken) or 'unscripted' (as in ordinary conversation), or indeed 'part scripted' (e.g. in broadcast media interviews, discussions and chat shows). The associated sub-discipline of linguistics is called 'discourse analysis'.

Text 篇章 / 文本

Usually used to refer to written structures above the level of the sentence, in contrast to (spoken) discourse; but some linguists have used the term to encompass both written and spoken material. Different approaches and techniques have, however, been developed to analyse and describe spoken discourse and written text. For this reason, and because the two terms are in use, there is some justification for restricting 'discourse' to speech and 'text' to writing. The associated sub-discipline of linguistics is called 'text linguistics'.

adjacency pair 相邻语对 / 邻近语对

A term from **conversation analysis**, referring to a sequence of utterances by two speakers in a conversation that form a matching pair, e.g. greeting – greeting, question – answer, offer – acceptance. The opening of the sequence is called the 'first pair part', and the closing the 'second pair part'. Normally, the first pair part would predict a 'preferred' second pair part; but a 'dispreferred' second pair part may occur, as in: 'Good morning, Jack' – 'What do you want?', where the initial greeting is not followed by the expected return greeting.

Anaphora 回指（照应）

The use of a pro-form, especially a third person pronoun (<u>he</u>, <u>she</u>, <u>it</u>, <u>they</u>), which refers back (anaphoric reference) in a text or discourse to a previously mentioned noun (phrase). For example, in 'The next train departs in ten minutes. We have no hope of catching it', <u>it</u> refers back (anaphorically) to <u>the next train</u> in the previous sentence. Anaphoric links of this kind contribute to the **cohesion** in a text. Compare **cataphora.**

Backchannel 反馈语 / 附和语

See **minimal response.**

Cataphora 后指（照应）

The use of a pro-form, e.g. a demonstrative pronoun (<u>this</u>), to point forward in a text to a noun (phrase) or other element yet to be mentioned. For example, in 'Listen to this. Lydia has won a prize', <u>this</u> refers forward to the information contained in the second sentence. Cataphoric links contribute to **cohesion**, but they occur much less frequently than **anaphora.**

Clause relation 语义单位关系 / 从句关系

A term coined by Eugene Winter to refer to the connections that we perceive between clauses as we try to make sense of a text. Clause relations may be signalled explicitly by means of one or more of: (a) subordinators (e.g. <u>although</u>), (b) conjuncts (e.g. <u>however</u>), (c) lexical signals (e.g. <u>reason</u>). Clause relations fall into two broad categories: **logical sequence** and **matching**.

Coherence 连贯

This refers to the conceptual sense that a text makes, such as in the development of ideas and arguments. Coherence is achieved by ensuring that sufficient links are present, or that the sequencing of information is such, that the reader is able to interpret the text as the writer intends. Compare **cohesion.**

Cohesion 衔接

The explicit links between sentences in a text, which bind the text together and create a textual structure. Cohesion may be 'grammatical' (e.g. **reference, conjunction, ellipsis, substitution**) or it may be 'lexical' (see **lexical cohesion**). The classic work on cohesion in English is Halliday & Hasan (1976).

Comment 论述 / 陈述 / 说明

The part of a sentence or utterance that says something about the **topic**, usually the 'new' or newsworthy part of the sentence, containing the **focus.**

Conjunction 连接词

A type of **cohesion** that uses conjunctions (<u>and,</u> <u>but</u>) or conjunctive adverbs (<u>however</u>, <u>moreover</u>, <u>nevertheless</u>) to signal relations between sentences in a text. Conjunctive relations may be categorized into: 'additive' (<u>and</u> relations), 'adversative' (<u>but</u> relations), 'temporal' (<u>then</u> relations), and 'causal' (<u>so</u> relations).

Context 语境

This usually refers to the situation in which a discourse or text is located, rather than the surrounding language as such. Compare **cotext**.

Conversation analysis 会话分析

An approach to spoken discourse whose main focus is 'talk in interaction'. Arising from the work of American sociologist Harvey Sacks in the 1960s, CA (as it is known) takes a fairly global view of a spoken interaction. It does not claim to account for every item, but rather concentrates on repeated patterns and their contribution to the developing organization of a discourse. Of particular concern are: **turn** taking and its management, **adjacency pairs**, how participants interpret a previous turn. An introductory text is Hutchby & Wooffitt (1988).

Cotext 共文 / 上下文

The surrounding words, sentences, or text of a stretch of language within a discourse or text, as compared with the situational **context**.

Critical discourse analysis 批评性话语分析 / 话语批评分析

An approach to the analysis of texts that investigates the language of texts with the purpose of uncovering their underlying ideology. Texts are seen as both reflecting the author's view of the world and an author's attempt to impose that view on the reader of the text. Using categories from a number of linguistic approaches (e.g. transitivity from systemic-functional grammar), CDA researchers make analyses of texts to expose the assumptions that the language encapsulates. With its origins in work at the University of East Anglia in the 1970s, CDA's most renowned recent exponent is Norman Fairdough at the University of Lancaster. See Fairclough (1995).

Discourse marker 话语标记（语）

An item such as <u>well</u> or <u>now</u>, coming at the beginning of an utterance and marking a boundary between one part of a spoken discourse and the next, i.e. signalling the start of a new section of the discourse. For example, 'Now, let's turn our attention to …'

Dysfluency 不流利（现象）

In spoken discourse, the normal phenomena that a speaker manifests as they compose what they want to say, including pauses, hesitations, false starts, incomplete sentences, and the like. These normal dysfluency features, which hearers mostly filter out, are to be distinguished from pathological dysfluencies, which are studied by speech and language pathologists (see Psycholinguistics section).

Ellipsis 省略

A grammatical device of **cohesion** that omits one or more elements of a sentence, leaving a gap that can be filled by 'recovering' the omitted element(s) from the previous sentence. It is more common in spoken discourse than in written text. For example, if one participant in a conversation says 'Where is she going?', and the other replies 'To town', then the reply contains ellipsis of <u>She is going</u>, which can be recovered from the question to which it is a reply. The ellipsis thus acts as a kind of **anaphora**.

Endophoric 内指/语内照应

Reference within a text, either by **anaphora** (backwards) or by **cataphora** (forwards). Compare **exophoric**.

Evaluation 评价

The inclusion in a text or discourse of items that reflect the attitude of the author towards what they are writing or saying. For example, prefacing a remark by <u>fortunately</u> implies that the author approves of what is about to be said. This has become an important research area in discourse and text linguistics in recent years; see Hunston & Thompson (2000).

Exchange 回合 / 交换

The crucial unit in the scheme of discourse analysis associated with the Birmingham School (John Sinclair and Malcolm Coulthard). It is composed of three potential **moves**: 'initiation', 'response' and 'feedback' (**IRF**). It relates to the **adjacency pair** of **conversation analysis**; but this approach to discourse analysis attempts to account for every item in a discourse and proposes a hierarchy of units (transaction-exchange-move-act) that parallels the sentence-clause-phrase-word hierarchy of syntax. For an up-to-date account, see Stenström (1994).

Exophoric 外指 / 语外照应

Reference by an item to something outside of the text. First and second person pronouns (I, you) usually have exophoric reference, to the speaker and addressee, respectively, by contrast with third person pronouns (he, she, it, they), which are normally **endophoric** and specifically **anaphoric**.

False start 起始话语失误

A normal **dysfluency** feature, when a speaker begins an utterance, has a change of mind and chooses to rephrase what they have begun to say. For example, 'This new procedure is … I haven't yet got my head around the new procedure'.

Filled pause 有声停顿 / 填充停顿

In spontaneous speech, a pause that is marked by a hesitation feature such as um, er, as against an 'unfilled pause', which is a brief moment of silence.

Floor-holding device 话轮持有策略 / 话语权保有策略

A tactic used by a speaker to ensure that they are able to keep talking (holding the floor) and so preventing an interlocutor from interrupting and gaining the floor. Floor-holding devices include: speeding up the rate of speaking, avoiding eye contact, using a conjunction (e.g. and) to indicate that there is more to come, raising the intonation pitch to signal incompleteness.

Focus 焦点

The most newsworthy element in a sentence, usually marked by the nucleus of an intonation unit (see Phonetics and Phonology section). It is what is most newsworthy about the **topic** of the sentence. In many texts, the information or argument is carried forward as the focus of one sentence becomes the topic of the following sentence, and so on.

Fronting 前置／前移

The movement to the beginning of a sentence of an element that would not normally occupy that position, for the purposes of enabling the message in a text to flow, or to create a contrast. For example, in 'This proposal I can support', the syntactic object this proposal has been fronted. Compare **postponement**.

General-particular 普遍—特殊／一般—特殊（模式）

A pattern regularly found in the structure of texts, beginning with some general statement, to which are then added some specifics. Hoey (1983) suggests that there are two patterns that fall into this category. The first is the 'Generalisation-Example' pattern, e.g. 'Ecosystems may be destroyed, either naturally or, more probably, through the interference of humans. For example, an ecosystem may be disturbed because one or more species are wiped out.' The second is the 'Preview-Detail' pattern, e.g. 'There are more than a million known living insect species and almost all of them have wings. Winged insects are further classified into two major groups on the basis of their developmental changes or metamorphosis.' Compare **problem-solution**.

Genre 体裁

A term with a variety of uses within different disciplines. In literature, it marks the basic distinction between prose fiction, poetry and drama, with their sub-genres, e.g. epic and lyric for poetry. More widely, the term is used to refer to different types of text/discourse, e.g. advertisement, legal document, news broadcast, soap opera, and so on. Care needs to be taken to ensure that, in a specific context, the scope of the term is clear. Compare **text type**.

Hedge 模糊限制语

A device of spoken discourse that a speaker uses in order to mitigate the effect of what they have to say, to make it sound less forceful and more polite. Hedges include expressions like <u>perhaps</u>, <u>maybe</u>, <u>to a certain extent</u>, as well as the teenager's <u>like</u> or <u>sort of</u>.

Intertextuality 互文性

Within a text, the inclusion of material from, or the allusion to, other texts. Introduced by the philosopher and literary critic Julia Kristeva in the 1960s, the term has been used in many different ways, encompassing notions such as 'allusion' and 'parody'. Within text linguistics, intertextuality is seen as contributing to **textuality**.

IRF (initiation – response – feedback)
三话步结构（引发－回答－反馈）

The three-part structure of an **exchange**: initiation – response – feedback, though the last part does not always occur. The original research that proposed this structure was carried out on classroom discourse in the 1960s, where an exchange between teacher and pupil would typically consist of two teacher turns (I, F) to one pupil turn (R). See Coulthard (1985).

Kinesics 身势学 / 体语学

The study of body language (as an aspect of non-verbal communication) during face-to-face interaction, including gestures, facial expressions, positioning of the body in relation to interlocutors.

Lexical cohesion 词汇衔接

A type of **cohesion** whereby linkages in texts are by means of lexical items (rather than grammatically), including: 'repetition' of a lexical item; use of a synonym; use of a collocate. Although looser than grammatical cohesion, these lexical links still contribute to the cohesion of a text.

Logical sequence 逻辑顺序（关系）

A type of **clause relation** that signals the development of successive events or ideas. Three types of logical sequence relation have been identified (Hoey 1983): condition-consequence (if X, then Y); instrument-achievement (X by means of Y); cause-consequence (X because Y). Compare **matching** relation.

Matching 对应（关系）

A type of **clause relation** that signals similarity or difference between the content of one sentence and that of the following one. Two types of matching relation have been identified (Hoey 1983): contrast (X, however Y) and compatibility (X, similarly Y).

Minimal response 最简回答 / 最简反馈

The usually one-word responses by a hearer in a conversation, often to indicate that they are paying attention. A minimal response could be either just Yes or No, but there is a range of other items that also occur, such as Right, Uh-hu, OK, and Really. Sometimes, such items are called 'backchannel'.

Move 话步

The constituent of an **exchange**, uttered as either an 'initiation', a 'response', or 'feedback'. Other types of move include 'frame' and 'focus', which are used to introduce a **transaction**.

Postponement 后置 / 后移

The moving of an element to the end of a sentence that would not normally be positioned there, for the purposes of improving the flow of information in a text. The end position is associated with **focus** and 'new' information; and there is a principle of 'end weight' operating in English that tends to send longer, more 'weighty' elements to the end of a sentence. For example, in 'I saw your cousin at the conference who you said that I should meet up with', the relative clause <u>who you said I should meet up with</u> has been detached from its antecedent noun (<u>cousin</u>) and postponed.

Problem-solution 问题—解决（模式）

A recurring pattern of organization found in texts, proposed by Hoey (1983), which is typically composed of the following slots: situation – problem – response – evaluation/result. Hoey's classic example is: 'I was on sentry duty' (situation) – 'I saw the enemy approaching' (problem) – 'I opened fire' (response) – 'I beat off the attack' (evaluation/result). Many texts use this basic pattern in their structuring. Compare **general-particular**.

Reference 指称

A type of grammatical **cohesion**, in which a pronoun refers either backwards (**anaphora** – the most usual case) or forwards (**cataphora**) in a text to a noun (phrase) in a neighbouring sentence. For example, in 'The gulls were wheeling above the lake. They were calling raucously to each other', <u>they</u> in the second sentence refers back to <u>the gulls</u> in the first.

Rhetoric 修辞 / 修辞学

In classical times (ancient Greece and Rome), instruction in the art of persuasion and effective public speaking. Now, rhetoric is the part of text linguistics (and pragmatics) that studies the linguistic construction of argument and the nature of persuasive language.

Substitution 替代 / 替换

A type of grammatical **cohesion**, in which a substitute form, typically one for noun phrases and so/not for clauses, replaces the associated unit in a previous sentence. For example, in 'The kids have just got the new computer game' – 'Mine have got one, too', one in the response substitutes the new computer game in the first sentence; in 'Has the train left yet?' – 'I don't think so', so in the response substitutes the whole of the first sentence, i.e. that the train has left yet.

Text type 文本类型

The characterization of texts on the basis of their internal features and structure, as well as their typical functions. The following general types may be distinguished: narrative, descriptive, expository, argumentative, and instructive (see Werlich 1976). Compare **genre**.

Textuality 篇章性 / 文本性

The features of text structure that constitute a sequence of sentences or utterances as a 'text' rather than a random collection, including **coherence**, **cohesion**, **intertextuality**, intentionality, informativity. See Beaugrande & Dressler (1981).

Topic 话题 / 主题

What is announced as being what a sentence (or paragraph, or text) is about, usually 'given' information (i.e. mentioned in previous text), and on which the rest of the linguistic unit is a **comment**, including the **focus**. How topics are introduced, how a text or discourse keeps track of topics, how topic change occurs, are all important factors in discourse/ text linguistics and the subject of considerable research. Languages have a variety of means by which they manage topics, including word order, specific particles or morphemes, intonation.

Transaction 课段

A unit in discourse analysis that is composed of a number of **exchanges**; a transaction would normally consist of a single topic and may be introduced by a 'framing' or 'focus' **move**.

TRP (transition relevance place) 转换关联位置

An acronym for 'transition relevance place'; a point at which a participant in a conversation who has the role of hearer deems that the current speaker may legitimately lose the floor (end their **turn**) and the hearer may take on the role of speaker. Where participants are competing for the floor (the role of speaker), being able to recognize TRPs is crucial for those who wish to make their voice heard. A variety of clues may signal a TRP, such as eye contact, a falling intonation, the end of a clause or sentence, body language.

Turn 话轮

The contribution of a single speaker to a developing spoken discourse. A **backchannel** is not normally considered to constitute a turn. In **conversation analysis**, the management of turns represents an important area of investigation, including how a turn is relinquished, **floor-holding devices**, how a speaker may allocate next turn, how a hearer knows when it is appropriate to take the floor (**TRP**).

Sociolinguistics

Sociolinguistics 社会语言学

This studies the ways in which language varies according to social context, e.g. who is speaking, the social situation, the occasion and purpose. Factors associated with a person's provenance, education, gender and socio-economic class influence the variety of language they speak. Thus, issues relating to accent and dialect interest sociolinguists, as do issues associated with societies that are multilingual. A growing topic of research is language and gender (information at: www. linguistics.ucsb.edu/faculty/bucholtz/lng/index.html).

Accent 口音

The distinctive pronunciation associated with a particular geographical area or social group. Accents may be distinguished at varying levels of generality: we may speak of the American accent as against the British accent, of the southern British accent (/kʌp/ and /grɑːs/ for <u>cup/grass</u>) as against the northern British accent (/kʊp/ and /græs/), of the West Midlands accent, the Black Country accent, etc. Accent is distinct from **dialect**; it refers only to features of pronunciation. The most prestigious accent of British English is 'received pronunciation' (**RP**), which is the accent usually given for the pronunciation of words in dictionaries.

Accommodation 适应／调节

The adjustment of your speaking style so that it becomes more similar to the person you are speaking to; also called 'convergence'. This may happen when talking to children, non-native speakers, or someone from a different dialect area.

Acrolect 高层语／高势语／上层方言

The prestigious, high (H) language variety used in a society with **diglossia**.

Affective function 情感功能

The use of language to express the speaker's attitude or feeling towards what they are saying, by contrast with the 'referential' function, which is about the content of what is said.

Attitude (to language) （语言）态度

How we react to other people's speech; this has been an important area of research, especially in relation to accents. See Ryan & Giles (1982).

Basilect 低层语／低势语／下层方言

The non-prestigious, low (L) language variety used in a society with **diglossia**.

Bilingualism 双语

The study of individuals and societies that speak two or more languages. Interest focuses on the relative **prestige** of the languages and on their differing roles within a society. For example, a designated **national language** will often be used for public communication, government, and secondary/tertiary education. There are many societies in the world that are bi-/ multilingual, probably more than are monolingual.

Black English 黑人英语

The varieties of English spoken by people of Afro-Caribbean origin, also called 'Black English Vernacular' (BEV). Compare **patois**.

Code 语码

The term used to denote the language or variety of language that is being used by a speaker in a particular social context, or that a speaker is able to use as part of their **linguistic repertoire**. Compare **speech**, **style**, **variety**.

Code switching 语码转换／转码

The insertion, usually by bilingual speakers, of a word or phrase from one language into an utterance that is basically constructed in another language; e.g. 'Could you come mañana?' where the Spanish word mañana 'tomorrow' is inserted into a basically English utterance. 'Code' may refer not to a language but to a dialect, where a word or phrase from one dialect is inserted into the speech of another.

Communicative competence 交际能力

The ability to take part in interactions within a **speech community**, which implies knowing more than the language (grammar, vocabulary, pronunciation), including norms of interaction, when it is appropriate to speak and to keep silent, the rules for turn taking, how to be polite, and so on.

Covert prestige 隐性声望

The standard dialect of a language normally has the highest **prestige** in a society, but it may be that a regional dialect has higher prestige for a particular social group, because it gives a sense of belonging and identity; the regional dialect then has covert prestige.

Dialect 方言

The variety of language, including vocabulary and grammar, spoken in a defined geographical area (regional dialect) or by a particular social group (social dialect). Interest in the past has focused on rural dialects, e.g. the Survey of English Dialects project of the 1950s (see: www.yorksj.ac.uk/ dialect/SED.htm), documentation and recordings from which are available at: www.collectbritain.co.uk/collections/dialects/. An attempt to include contemporary urban dialects can be found in the BBC's 'Voices' project (see: www.bbc.co.uk/voices). A survey of American English dialects has been published in the *Dictionary of American Regional English* (see: http://polyglot.lss.wisc.edu/dare/dare.html).

Dialect continuum 方言连续体 / 方言连续性 / 方言渐变

The notion that, while dialects at either end of a country may not be mutually intelligible, those that are geographically contiguous will be, thus providing a continuum of mutual intelligibility across dialects of a language.

Diglossia 双言现象

A society where there are two language varieties, one of high **prestige** (usually designated 'H') and one of lower prestige (designated 'L'); they are usually varieties of the same language (e.g. Standard Arabic and Colloquial Arabic), though they may be different languages [e.g. French and Alsatian (a dialect of German) in the Alsace region of France]. The H variety is usually used for public communication and education, while the L variety is largely only spoken. The term **acrolect** is sometimes used for the H variety, and **basilect** for the L variety; if there is a third, intermediate, form, it is called a 'mesolect'.

Domain 领域

Typical contexts of use that may determine the language variety chosen, e.g. family, religion, education, employment.

Elaborated code 精制代码 / 完备代码

A term coined by the sociologist Basil Bernstein to refer to the variety of language spoken by educated, middle-class people; it does not rely on the immediate context for its interpretation (compare **restricted code**), but is elaborated in the sense that its language is explicit in its reference, e.g. using nouns rather than pronouns, and using adjectives and other modifiers to expand on noun reference.

Elicitation 诱导法

A common method of data collection in sociolinguistics, and especially in **dialect** studies, usually involving a questionnaire that is administered to a sample of relevant subjects in order to elicit from them the forms of speech under investigation.

Formality 正式程度

A dimension of variation that influences the **speech style** of language or **code** that may be used, along a spectrum from very informal or colloquial to very formal or frozen.

High variety 高标准语言 /H 语言
low variety 低标准语言 /L 语言

In a situation of **diglossia**, the difference between a language or variety of language that is used for 'high' purposes such as government or education and one that is used for 'low' purposes such as interaction within the family or friendship group; abbreviated to 'H' and 'L'. The high variety usually has more **prestige**.

Hypercorrection 过度纠正 / 矫枉过正

Usage, usually by a low status speaker, that exceeds the norm that is part of the **standard** variety. For example, the between you and I (instead of me) phenomenon is thought to be due to hypercorrection.

Idiolect 个人语言

The characteristics of the speech of an individual, as against a **dialect**, which refers to a geographical or social group.

Isogloss 同言线 / 同语线 / 等语线

A line drawn on a **dialect** map, indicating the boundary of some feature. For example the /æ/ – /ɑː/ isogloss in England distinguishes the midlands and northern pronunciation of words like <u>grass</u> from the southern one. A bundle of isoglosses in the same area indicates a firm dialect boundary.

Jargon 行话

The variety of language associated with a particular profession, craft, sport, etc. Jargon is largely a matter of specialist vocabulary, e.g. <u>lesion</u> in medicine, <u>U-bend</u> in plumbing, <u>fine leg</u> in cricket.

Language 语言

A problematical term, especially in relation to **dialect**. What constitutes a language is often a matter of its speakers' perception or the boundaries of the nation state. For example. Norwegian, Swedish and Danish are, to an extent, mutually intelligible; but they are considered separate languages, rather than part of a dialect continuum, because they are the national languages of separate states. Is Scots, for example, a separate language, or a dialect of English? (See www.scotslanguage.com)

Language maintenance 语言保持
language shift 语言更替

The retention of a **minority language** (e.g. by immigrant communities) over against the language of the majority (i.e. maintenance) as against the adoption of the language of the host community (i.e. shift).

Language planning 语言规划

This is usually undertaken by an official body, e.g. a language academy or a language board, with the aim of regulating language use within a society. It may involve deciding which languages are to be used for which functions in society, or deciding on new terms that should be added to the language. For example, language planning in respect of the Welsh language, including the standardization of terminology in Welsh, has been undertaken by the Welsh Language Board (www.welsh-language-board.org.uk).

Lingua franca 通用语

The language of communication between persons who have different first languages; for example, in East Africa, Swahili is often used as a lingua franca for those who speak different tribal languages.

Linguistic repertoire 全部语言变体 / 交际语库

The range of **codes** or **variet**ies (e.g. languages, dialects, styles) that are available to a speaker to choose from in any social context.

Minority language 少数民族语言 / 少数族裔语言

The language spoken by a minority group within a country, e.g. because of border changes (such as Hungarians in Romania), or because of historical development (such as Bretons in France), or because of immigration (such as Panjabi speakers in the UK).

National language 国家语言

The language adopted by a country, usually as a symbol of national unity and for public communication, e.g. Swahili in Tanzania. Some states, e.g. India or South Africa, do not have a national language but a number of **official language**s.

Observer's paradox 观察者悖论

The insight of William Labov that, when an investigator attempts to collect 'natural' speech from an informant or group of informants, their presence influences the way in which the informants speak, often leading to **hypercorrection** on the part of the informants. The 'paradox' is that an investigator has to be present to collect speech samples, but their very presence affects the samples they are wanting to collect.

Official language 官方语言

A language designated by a state for use in public communication, education, etc. South Africa has eleven official languages (see http://salanguages.com/); India has two (Hindi and English) at national level, while each state has its own official language(s). Compare **national language**, **vernacular**.

Patois （黑人）土语/土话

A term used to denote the variety of English (creole) used by **Black English** speakers.

Pidgins 洋泾浜语　　creoles 克里奥语

A pidgin forms when speakers of two different languages create a restricted form of speech based on elements from both their languages, as a means of essential communication. Many pidgins arose as a consequence of colonization and slavery. Most pidgins have one of the European colonial languages as one of their inputs – English, French, Spanish, Portuguese. A pidgin is not one's native language; when it develops to the extent that it is routinely acquired as a native language, then it becomes a creole, and it may undergo processes of expansion, stabilization and **standard**ization. Tok Pisin, widely spoken in Papua New Guinea, was a pidgin that developed into a creole: newspapers are published in Tok Pisin, there is a translation of the Bible, and it is used in the PNG parliament.

Power 权力 / 权势

The power relationship between participants in an interaction affects the language of both parties. It will affect how each addresses the other, e.g. Title + Last Name (TLN), First Name (FN), and it will affect the formality of the language used. Contrast **solidarity**.

Prestige 特权 / 强势 / 声望

The status that a dialect or a language has within a society. Normally, the standard variety is the one with prestige, since it is used for public communication, as the medium of education, and it is taught to foreign learners. If someone aspires to speak the standard variety, they are engaging in 'overt prestige'. But there is also prestige associated with speaking a non-standard dialect, since it reinforces group membership and social identity; someone who adopts a non-standard variety engages in **covert prestige**.

Register 语域

A term used either to denote the **jargon** associated with a particular occupational group, or more widely to refer to any **variety** that is influenced by subject matter, **setting**, group being addressed, and so on.

Restricted code 限制性代码

The language variety spoken, according to sociologist Basil Bernstein, by members of the 'working class'. It is characterized by having reference only to its immediate context of utterance, especially by the use of pronouns, rather than noun phrases. Contrast **elaborated code**. Since elaborated code is the variety used in education, speakers of restricted code are said to be at an educational disadvantage.

RP (received pronunciation) 标准发音

The prestigious accent of British English. It derives from the speech of 'public' (i.e. private) schools in southern England, as documented originally by Daniel Jones in the *English Pronouncing Dictionary* (1917); it is not restricted to a particular region; it is the accent used for pronunciation information in British English dictionaries; and it is generally the model for learners of British English as a foreign language.

Setting 场合

The location or situational context where an interaction takes place, e.g. home, school, church, place of work, and which may influence the variety of language used.

Social distance 社会距离

A dimension of variation relating to the level of intimacy between participants in an interaction, on a scale from 'distant' to 'intimate'. The more 'intimate' the relationship between the participants, the greater will be the degree of **solidarity**. Compare **status**.

Social network 社交网络

The variety of groups within a **speech community** that we interact with and that defines our social identity; we may adopt different **speech style**s according to which group we are communicating with.

Solidarity 一致性 / 等同关系

The relationship between interlocutors of equal status, with its consequent effect on the language used, e.g. in terms of address. Contrast **power**.

Speech community 言语社区

A group of people who speak a common language, **dialect** or other language variety. Speech communities are often recognized on geographical or ethnic criteria, but the term is as vague as is that of dialect and needs to be carefully defined.

Speech function 言语功能

The purpose of a speech event encoded in the language. Broadly, utterances exhibit to varying degrees a 'referential' and an **affective** function; e.g. 'I love her dearly' is more 'affective' than 'There is a bond of affection between her and me'. Sociolinguists sometimes operate with a more differentiated set of speech functions, e.g. 'expressive', 'directive', 'poetic', 'phatic'.

Speech style 言语风格

The variety of ways of speaking that we adopt according to the persons we are interacting with; we talk in different ways to our close friends, our work colleagues, officials in positions of power, and so on.

Standard 标准（语）

A prestigious, high variety of a language, used for public communication, education, published documents, and taught to foreign learners of the language. The standard has an agreed form of spelling, grammar and vocabulary; but the standard may be spoken with any **accent**. In reality, the grammar and vocabulary of the standard, and to a limited extent the spelling, do exhibit a measure of variation and do change over time.

Status 地位 / 身份

A dimension of variation that refers to the **power** relationship between participants in an interaction and may affect the language variety that is used in the interaction. Status can be viewed as on a scale from 'superior' to 'inferior' or subordinate. Compare **social distance**.

Variable 变量 / 变项

A linguistic feature that is hypothesized to correlate with a social variable (e.g. gender, socio-economic group). For example, -ing (as in feeling) might be pronounced /ɪŋ/ or /ɪn/, which may correlate with both gender and socio-economic group in England.

Variation 变异

The focus of sociolinguistics, charting how language varies, and matching variation in language to social contexts and social group membership. The dimensions of variation include: geography, age, gender, socio-economic status, power relations, etc.

Variety 变体

The general term used to denote a form of language (pronunciation, grammar, vocabulary) that is used by particular social groups in particular social contexts. It includes **dialect**, **jargon**, **register**, etc.

Vernacular 本地话 / 本土语

This term is sometimes used to refer to a local, non-standardized language, such as may be learnt first by a child. It is also used in a wider sense to refer to any language that is not designated as an **official language**. More widely still, it may refer to any colloquial variety used by a speaker, as against the **standard**.

Psycholinguistics

Psycholinguistics 心理语言学

The interface between psychology and linguistics. It studies language in the individual, including: how language is acquired, how language is stored in the brain, how language is accessed and processed by the brain, what happens when there is language loss (**aphasia**), the processes involved in learning a second language, and so on.

Animal communication 动物交流 / 动物交际

This is studied by psycholinguists in comparison with human language, to determine the degree to which animal and human communication systems are similar or different. Charles Hockett (1916-2000) proposed a number of **design features** of human language, which, taken together, are not shared by any animal communication system. Animal communication that has attracted particular attention has included bee dancing, dolphin whistles, and whale song. Attempts to teach human language to primates, especially chimpanzees, has attained only very limited success after a great expenditure of effort.

Aphasia 失语症

Impairment in the use of language, caused by damage to the brain as a result of a stroke, accident, etc. Different types of aphasia are recognized, depending on the part of the brain that has suffered damage, e.g. Broca's aphasia, which is manifest in a loss of syntax and inflections; and Wernicke's aphasia, which is fluent but lacks coherence. The study of aphasics has been important in gaining understanding of how the brain stores and processes language.

Articulation rate 发音速度

The rate at which speech (sounds) are produced, excluding any pauses. It is usually expressed as syllables per second, typically between 4.4 and 5.9 syllables per second in English. The typical rates vary from language to language, depending on syllable structures. Compare **speaking rate**.

Behaviourism 行为主义

The dominant view in psychology in the first half of the twentieth century that behaviour was entirely learned, by means of 'conditioning' on the basis of responses to stimuli. This included 'verbal behaviour', i.e. language. It was considered idle to speculate on the mind, and in general thought was considered to be dependent on language. The most famous exponent of this view was B. F. Skinner (1904-90), whose book *Verbal Behaviour* (1957) was subjected to a trenchant critique by Noam Chomsky in a review published in the linguistics journal *Language* (1959).

Concept 概念

What a word refers to. Psycholinguistics is interested in how concepts are stored in the mind and how related concepts are distinguished, especially where boundaries between concepts are fuzzy or where they overlap. Compare **prototype**.

Connectionism 联结主义

A theory, based on the operation of neural connections in the brain, which suggests that the more a 'connection' is used, the stronger it becomes, and vice versa. For example, the lexical connection between <u>lawn</u> and <u>mow</u> is stronger than that between, say, <u>tree</u> and <u>grass</u>, because the first pair is more frequently found together.

Critical period （语言）关键期 / 临界期

The period in a child's life, up to the onset of puberty, in which a child is said to be capable of acquiring full command of a first language. It is also thought that the acquisition or learning of a second language should ideally fall within this period. The brain loses some of its flexibility at puberty. This means that children deprived of language up to that point are unlikely to acquire it in any full sense (see **feral/attic children**), and a second language learned after the critical period is rarely acquired with native-like competence.

Design features （语言的）设计特征 / 识别特征 / 结构特征

A set of a dozen or so characteristics of all human languages not found together in any **animal communication** system. Some of the more significant include: 'arbitrariness' – no logical relation between the form (spelling or pronunciation) and the meaning of a word or utterance; 'displacement' – language can refer to things remote in time and space; 'productivity' – language users can create and understand messages that are novel and have not before been uttered; 'duality of patterning' – sounds combine into words, and words combine into sentences. For a full list, see Hockett (1966), or www.ling.ohio-state.edu/~swinters/371/designfealures.html.

Dysgraphia 书写困难症 / 书写障碍症

Either the delayed acquisition of writing skills, or their loss as a result of impairment of the brain. It is often related to **dyslexia**.

Dyslexia 阅读困难症 / 阅读障碍症

A range of phenomena associated with either the delay in acquiring or the non-acquisition of skills of reading (and writing — see **dysgraphia**) or their loss as a result of brain damage or impairment. It is manifested in difficulties with reading (associating letters with sounds), spelling, and writing. Up to one-tenth of the population is estimated to suffer from some sort of dyslexia. See the website of the British Dyslexia Association: www.bdadyslexia.org.uk. Information can also be found at Dyslexia Action's website: www.dyslexiaaction.org.uk.

Feral children 野生儿童   attic children 阁楼儿童

Both types suffer from language deprivation during the **critical period**. Feral children, like the fictional Mowgli in Rudyard Kipling's *The Jungle Book*, grow up in the wild without human contact. The most famous real instance was Victor, the 'Wild Boy of Aveyron' in France, discovered in 1800. Attic children are deprived of human contact by their parents or other caregivers and so receive no language stimulus; the most famous case is that of Genie in the USA, discovered in 1970 at the age of 13. Further information can be found at: www.feralchildren.com/en/index. php.

Frame 框架

Knowledge about the world and the language associated with it may be stored in our minds as a 'frame', with appropriate 'slots'. For example, a frame for house would contain slots for kitchen, lounge, bathroom, bedroom, front door, garden, etc., which would be activated when we read or hear the word house. See also: **schema, script**.

Garden path sentence 花园小径句 / 庭院路径句

A sentence that is difficult to process when heard, because its ending does not relate to expectations raised by its beginning. For example, the opening The lawyer questioned ... raises expectations of a direct object (someone whom the lawyer questions), so that the ending <u>... by the judge admitted lying</u> is against expectations. The hearer has been led 'up the garden path'. Such sentences provide insight into the ways in which we process speech.

LAD (language acquisition device) 语言习得机制

Associated with Chomsky's **mentalist** theory of acquisition, the innate device in a human being that enables language acquisition to take place. Language input is said to trigger LAD, which oversees the acquisition of the specific language. The theory has been superseded by the notion that children are born with **universal grammar**, which comprises features common to languages generally.

Language acquisition 语言习得

The term usually used of, and sometimes confined to, the acquisition by a child of their first language. The term is also used of 'second language acquisition' (**SLA**), which, in bilingual children, may occur at the same time as first language acquisition. The contrastive term is 'language learning', which refers to the acquisition of a second or subsequent language, usually in an educational setting, and implies instruction.

Lateralization 大脑偏侧化 / 大脑偏侧性

The theory that different functions are located in either the left side or the right side of the brain (see **localization**). Evidence suggests that damage to the left side of the brain affects language more severely than damage to the right side. However, if the damage occurs during the **critical period**, the language function seems to be able to relocate to the right side of the brain.

Lexical access 词汇通达

This refers to the processes that we use to access words in our **mental lexicon**. One theory would suggest that we use a process similar to a dictionary lookup, trailing through the list until we find the one we want. Other theories suggest that we use a more sophisticated process, which takes account of both the form (spelling/pronunciation) and the meaning of the word being accessed.

Localization （语言）区位化 / 定位化

The theory that the language faculty is localized in specific areas of the brain. On the basis of studies of **aphasia**, it was assumed, for example, that Broca's area (front left) controlled syntax, and Wernicke's area (back left) controlled vocabulary and comprehension. The recent use of 'imaging' techniques, e.g. with MRI (magnetic resonance imaging) scanning, suggests that language processing is spread much more widely across the areas of the brain.

Memory 记忆

A distinction is made between 'short-term memory' (or 'working memory'), which is a temporary store for immediate processing purposes, and 'long-term memory', which is where we store linguistic items (knowledge) for future access. It is suggested that we may have a further memory, a 'sensory store', which is divided into 'iconic memory' (for visual impressions) and 'echoic memory' (for auditory impressions); this is a very short-term memory, used for holding visual and auditory impressions while they are being matched against a stored pattern.

Mentalism 心智主义 / 心灵主义

The approach, especially to **language acquisition**, championed by Noam Chomsky in opposition to **behaviourism**, that the capacity for language is innate in human beings. The argument is that children could not possibly achieve the competence in language that they have by the age of five on the basis of the stimulus-response model of behaviourism. Chomsky posited an innate 'language acquisition device' (**LAD**), which supports a child's acquisition of language. Behaviourism allowed only observable data to be the object of linguistic investigation; mentalism investigates the mental and cognitive processes involved in language acquisition and use. This is the basis of cognitive linguistics.

Mental lexicon 心理词库

The lexical units (morphemes, words, expressions) that we have stored in our brains. Psycholinguists are interested in how lexical units are stored, e.g. the role of form (pronunciation/spelling) and the role of meaning in organizing our mental lexicons. They are also interested in how we access the stored units (**lexical access**). A further factor is the distinction between 'passive' vocabulary – words that we recognize – and 'active' vocabulary – words that we use in speech and writing; our passive vocabulary is always larger than our active one. If you are bilingual, then you store the lexical units of two or more languages; psycholinguistics is interested in the structure of the mental lexicon in bilinguals, e.g. whether separate mental lexicons exist for the two languages.

Nativism （语言）天赋论 / 先天论 / 先验论

The theory that the capacity for language is innate and is transmitted genetically from one generation to the next. Compare **mentalism**.

Neuro-linguistics 神经语言学

An inter-disciplinary field of study that is concerned with the mechanisms and processes in the brain that relate to the knowledge and use of language.

Over-generalization 过度概括 / 泛化

The process in language acquisition by which a child applies a newly acquired feature beyond its scope in adult language. For example, when the past tense suffix -ed is first acquired, it is applied to all verbs indiscriminately, including those common verbs that form their past tense irregularly, so catched for caught, seed for saw, drinked for drank.

The term is also applied to the acquisition of word meaning, where a child will over-extend the application of a newly acquired word, e.g. dog refers to all four-legged animals.

Pattern recognition 模式识别

In hearing and reading, the process of matching an auditory or visual signal with the representation (pattern) of a word or phrase that is stored in our brain.

Pivot grammar 枢轴语法 / 基础语法

A theory, proposed by M. D. S. Braine, that the two-word utterances of early child language acquisition can be analysed into a 'pivot' word and an 'open' word. There is a small number of pivots, also called 'operators', and a larger number of open words. For example, in more cake, more is the pivot word and cake the open word; in drink allgone, allgone is the pivot. So, pivots may precede or follow open words.

Priming 启动

The notion that the use of one word activates, or 'primes', the use of associated words, so that the latter are then more quickly recognized and processed. For example, teacher primes words like pupil/student, lesson, class, and so on. More recent research (Hoey 2005) suggests that priming is widespread in language processing, encompassing grammar as well as vocabulary. Compare **schema**.

Prototype 原型

The theory that we store in our minds images of **concepts** that contain the typical or salient features, and that we then relate other words on the basis of how well they fit with the prototype. For example, we may have a prototype concept of a 'bird', and when we come across a new word that may relate to this category, we try and make a best fit, e.g. with ostrich – it has feathers and walks on two legs, but it doesn't fly. The theory is particularly associated with the work of Eleanor Rosch, e.g. Rosch (1983).

Reading 阅读

Psycholinguistic research into the process of reading has investigated areas such as eye movement, the use of memory, readers' ability to predict, backtracking, the role of context, and so on. Interest has focused on what makes a successful reader – someone who can read quickly and fluently, and also understand a text's intended meaning.

Schema 图式

The stored knowledge that a person has about a particular **concept**, which enables them to interpret what they encounter in relation to that concept. For example, we might have a 'schema' associated with the concept 'school', with which would be associated: teachers, classes, headteacher, lessons, examinations, reading and writing, learning, etc. Related to schemas are **frames** and **scripts**.

Script 脚本

Within a **schema**, a script is a process associated with the **concept**, our expectations of the kinds of things that happen, which we have stored in our brains. For example, within the 'school' schema, a script could represent a typical lesson: teacher settles class, introduces topic of the lesson, gives explanation, asks questions, evaluates pupils' responses, gets pupils to undertake associated work, sums up topic, dismisses class.

Self-repair 自我修复 / 自修复

The ability of a speaker to backtrack and correct an error in speech that they have uttered. It implies that, as we speak, we monitor what we say, and so are able to effect repairs to what we recognize as a defective utterance.

SLA (second language acquisition) 二语习得

The acquiring or learning of a second language, either simultaneously with the first, in infancy, or subsequently, in later childhood or adulthood. SLA has been extensively researched, especially in the context of English as a second language, and theories of second language acquisition/learning abound. See Mitchell & Myles (2006).

Slips of the tongue 口误

These have been important for psycholinguists as a source of evidence for mental processes involved in **speech production**. Well-known types include 'spoonerisms' ('Drive into the par cark') and 'malapropisms' ('What are you incinerating?' for <u>insinuating</u>). They provide clues, for example, to how we associate words in our **mental lexicon**.

Speaking rate 语速

The rate at which a speaker utters a stretch of speech, including pauses, hesitations, and the like. Speakers vary widely, with a norm for English speakers of somewhere around 200 words a minute. Compare **articulation rate**.

Speech perception 言语感知

Psycholinguists are interested in how we process speech as hearers and decoders; whether we concentrate primarily on the sounds, whether we take context into account, whether we are attempting to predict what a speaker is saying. It seems likely that all these factors, and others, play a part in our perception of speech.

Speech production 言语产出

As the counterpart to **speech perception**, this investigates the processes that operate for us as speakers: how we get from the message in our minds to its articulation in speech. Issues of relevance here include **lexical access** and selection, the role of our internal grammar in structuring the message, and its conversion into speech sounds.

Spreading activation　激活扩散

In **connectionism**, the idea that the encounter with one word (e.g. theatre) activates associative links to related words, which are then recognized and processed more readily (e.g. play, actor, stage, scene, interval).

Thought and language　思维与语言

Controversy has long raged among philosophers, psychologists and linguists about the relationship between thought and language. **Behaviourists** would maintain that thought is impossible without language; **mentalist**s and cognitive linguists would argue for a measure of independence, and certainly that non-verbal thought is possible. Clearly, there is an important relationship, and the debate will continue, as further research is undertaken to support one position or another.

Tip of the tongue　舌尖现象

Not being able to think of a word to denote some **concept**. Tip of the tongue experiments give subjects a definition and ask them to provide the word, as a means of investigating lexical storage and **lexical access**.

Universal grammar　普遍语法

The notion that human beings are born with the features that are common to languages generally 'hard-wired' into their brains, i.e. they are innate. Part of the acquisition process for a child is to select those features that are relevant to the language input that they are receiving. Universal grammar gives children the mechanism they need to successfully engage in the language acquisition process. Compare **LAD**.

Word association 词语联想

A frequently used test in psycholinguistics, in which a subject is asked, when they are presented with a stimulus word, to say the first word that comes into their mind. The test intends to investigate how words are stored in our **mental lexicon**, e.g. by how they sound, or by relations of meaning, etc.

Working memory 工作记忆

Now the preferred term for 'short-term **memory**', the temporary store used in language processing.

Historical linguistics

Historical linguistics 历史语言学

This studies the origins and development of languages; the genetic relationships between languages; language change, including phonological, grammatical and semantic, and the reasons for it; the origins and development of words (**etymology**). The nineteenth century was the great era of historical linguistics, or **comparative philology**, but it is still an area of much scholarly activity. Its assumptions are that all languages are continually changing, that change is systematic, and that change may be due to social and cultural factors as well as linguistic ones.

Adstratum 附层（语言）/ 傍层（语言）

In a situation of language contact, where one language borrows words from a neighbouring language, often mutally, e.g. French and Flemish in Belgium. Compare **substratum**, **superstratum**.

Analogy 类比　　**anomaly** 异化 / 异体

Language change tends towards regularization, by analogy; irregularities are considered to be cases of 'anomaly'. For example, in some dialects of English, irregular (anomalous) past tenses of common verbs are regularized by analogy with the majority suffix -ed (seed for saw, teached for taught).

Attested form 有证形式

A word etc. of an ancient language that has been identified in a surviving manuscript or inscription, as against a 'reconstructed form' on the basis of the **comparative method**.

Cognate 同源词

A word in one language that is similar in form (spelling/pronunciation) and meaning to a word in another language, but has not been subject to borrowing. For example, dove in English is cognate with Taube in German, sleep is cognate with Dutch slaap. Cognates provide important clues to the genetic relatedness of languages and are crucial to the **comparative method**.

Comparative method 比较法 / 比照法

Used to establish relationships between languages by carefully comparing **cognate**s across a number of languages hypothesized to be related (see **Jones**). This method led to the establishment of the **Indo-European language family** in the nineteenth century and the **reconstruction** of supposed ancestors to living languages (including Indo-European itself).

Convergence 语言趋同

In situations of language contact, where there may be a large number of bilingual people, the borrowing of morphological and syntactic features, so that neighbouring languages become structurally more similar. On a larger scale, this may lead over time to a 'Sprachbund' or linguistic area, where unrelated languages converge. An example is the Balkan Sprachbund, in which Albanian, Romanian, Bulgarian and Macedonian show some convergence.

Diachronic 历时的

From Greek, literally 'through time', the historical approach to language study, which investigates the changes in languages through time. 'Diachronic' contrasts with 'synchronic', the study of a language at a point in time, which could be contemporary or at a period in past time.

Dialectology 方言学

In the study of contemporary languages, dialectology is the province of sociolinguistics, but it is also important in historical linguistics, especially as dialects at one time in history may either develop to become separate languages (e.g. the dialects of Latin that became today's Romance languages) or merge into a single language (e.g. the dialects of the Anglo-Saxon invaders of England in the fifth century that became English).

Diffusion （词汇）扩散

Also called 'lexical diffusion', the gradual and systematic spread of a sound change that began in a few words to all the relevant words in a language's vocabulary. Diffusion may also refer to the spread of a linguistic change throughout a speech community; starting with one social group, it diffuses to other groups within the community. The extent of the diffusion may depend on the prestige of the initiating group.

Drift 沿流

The term used for a perceived direction in the historical development of a language, e.g. from a synthetic (inflecting) language to an analytical one (without inflections, but, for example, with auxiliary verbs and prepositions).

Ethnologue 民族语言网

A print and web-based publication that gives details of all the languages

in the world, arranged in their **language families**. Go to www.
ethnologue.com.

Etymology 词源学

The study of the origins and development of words, including the
development of their form (usually spelling) and of their meaning.
Etymology makes a major contribution to historical lexicography, as
represented, for example, by the *Oxford English Dictionary* (www.oed.
com).

External history （语言的）外在历史
internal history （语言的）内在历史

The external history of a language refers to social and cultural factors
affecting its development; the internal history relates to changes
taking place in the features of the language itself, e.g. its phonology,
morphology, lexis and syntax. There may, of course, be some relation
between a language's external history and its internal development.

Glottochronology 语言年代学 / 词源统计分析法

A technique that uses statistical methods to investigate the vocabularies
of languages that are historically related, aiming to determine the degree
of relatedness between languages and the point at which they began to
develop separately.

Grammaticalization 语法化

The development of a word from one having an independent lexical
meaning to one that is used for grammatical purposes, and so losing its
lexical meaning. For example, the verb <u>have</u> developed into an auxiliary
verb indicating perfective aspect ('I have seen the play'), where it loses
its 'possession' meaning.

Grimm's Law 格林姆定律 / 格里姆定律

The first formulation of a regular sound change, proposed by Jakob Grimm in 1822 to account for regular consonantal changes in the **Indo-European** language family that led to the development of the Germanic languages. He noted, for example, that voiceless stops (plosives) became voiceless fricatives: compare Latin <u>pater</u> and English <u>father</u> (/p/ to /f/), Latin <u>tres</u> and English <u>three</u> (/t/ to /θ/), Latin <u>centum</u> and English <u>hundred</u> (/k/ to /h/).

Indo-European 印欧语系

The postulated ancestor of the majority of the languages of Europe and the northern part of the Indian sub-continent (e.g. Hindi/Urdu, Panjabi, Gujarati, Bengali). It was reconstructed on the basis of the **comparative method** by historical linguists of the nineteenth century. Work on establishing Indo-European was given a great boost by the work of Sir William **Jones** in the 1780s on Sanskrit, the ancient language of north India.

Isolate 孤立语

A language that it has not been possible for historical linguistics to assign to a language family. The most famous example in Europe is Basque, spoken in northern Spain and south-western France, which is reckoned to predate the arrival of Indo-European languages in Europe.

Jones (Sir William Jones) 琼斯（威廉·琼斯爵士）

Sir William Jones was a judge in the British colonial administration of India. In 1786, he gave a paper to the Royal Asiatic Society in Calcutta, in which he presented his research, including on Sanskrit, the ancient language of north India, which demonstrated the relatedness of Sanskrit to Latin, Greek, Gothic and Celtic; and he postulated that they had a common ancestor. This discovery gave a boost to the development of historical linguistics and the **comparative method,** and eventually to the

reconstruction of proto-lndo-European.

Language family 语族

A group of languages, established by the **comparative method**, that are related to each other historically. The major language families in the world are: Afro-Asiatic, Austronesian, **Indo-European**, Niger-Congo, Sino-Tibetan, Trans-NewGuinea. There are a further 100 or so smaller families. See **ethnologue**.

Mutation 元音变化 / 音变

A sound change in a word to effect a morphological change, e.g. the formation of past tense and past participles in verbs like <u>sing</u> – <u>sang</u> – <u>sung</u>, which is also called 'ablaut', by contrast with 'umlaut' (vowel fronting), e.g. singular <u>man</u> to plural <u>men</u>, or German <u>Sohn</u> 'son' to <u>Söhne</u> 'sons'.

Neo-grammarians 新语法学派

A group of historical linguists (called 'Junggrammatiker' in German) working in Leipzig, Germany, in the 1870s, who formulated the view that laws of sound change operate like laws of nature in their systematic application. Any exceptions were to be accounted for on the basis of **analogy**. They viewed the phonological level as the most important, and independent of the levels of syntax and semantics.

Paleolinguistics (linguistic paleontology) 语言化石学

The use of evidence from language to make deductions about the culture of (distant) past communities. For example, because there do not seem to be many words for metals that are shared by modern **Indo-European** languages, it is deduced that proto-Indo-European society existed before the discovery of metals. The methods and conclusions drawn by paleolinguistics are often disputed.

Philology 语文学 / 文献学

The study of the texts and cultural monuments of the past, with the aim of discovering the language and culture of these societies. 'Comparative philology' became historical linguistics in the nineteenth century, when scholars began to concentrate solely on using texts to trace language origins and development.

Proto-language 原始语 / 原语言

A reconstructed language, using the **comparative method**, which is assumed to be the ancestor of related languages that are attested through surviving texts. For example, Proto-Germanic is said to be the ancestor of languages such as Norwegian, Swedish, Danish, Dutch, German, Frisian, English, and Gothic (which is now extinct).

Reconstruction （内部）重构法 / 拟测法

Also termed 'internal reconstruction', it is the process by which a **proto-language** is established. Words common to the descendants are assumed to have constituted the vocabulary of the proto-language, and examination of sound changes and grammatical changes leads to the formulation of the proto-language's phonology and grammar.

Semantic change 语义变化

The processes by which the meanings of words develop over time. The meaning may become narrower or more restricted, e.g. English meat used to denote food in general, but is now restricted to the flesh of animals eaten for food. The meaning may become broader or more general, e.g. clerk originally had an exclusively religious meaning (clerk in holy orders), whereas it is now used of anyone whose job involves writing (clerk to the committee). The meaning may become more positive, or ameliorate, e.g. knight originally meant 'servant' but came to designate someone of status. The meaning may become more negative, or pejorative, e.g. propaganda originally had a religious use in relation to the spreading of the faith, whereas it is now used almost exclusively in a disapproving manner.

Sound shift 语音演变 / 语音变化

The process by which a systematic change takes place over time in the pronunciation of words. For example, the first Germanic consonant shift, encapsulated in **Grimm's Law**, affected the pronunciation of Germanic languages by comparison with that of Latin-derived Romance languages. In English, the Great Vowel Shift at the end of the medieval period introduced systematic changes in pronunciation, e.g. mice /miːs/ became /maɪs/, geese /geːs/ became /giːs/.

Stammbaum model 谱系树理论

The view that languages are related to each other in a family tree (German Stammbaum), e.g. that English, German and Dutch are 'daughters' of West Germanic, whose 'parent' is Primitive Germanic, which is a daughter of Proto-Indo-European. Compare **wave model**.

Substratum 底层语言

In a situation of language contact and lexical borrowing, the less prestigious language, perhaps that of a conquered people. For example, when the Anglo-Saxons invaded England, the developing English language borrowed a few words from the substratum Celtic language of the indigenous people, e.g. brock for 'badger', combe for 'valley', as in place names like Wycombe (valley of the River Wye). Compare **adstratum, superstratum**.

Superstratum 上层语言

In a situation of language contact and lexical borrowing, the more prestigious language, perhaps that of a conquering people. In England from 1066 onwards, (Norman) French formed a superstratum, and thousands of words were borrowed into English as the conquerors in due course acquired English. Compare **adstratum, substratum.**

Typology 语言类型学

By a comparison of the structures of the world's languages, grouping them into 'types' on the basis of shared features. For example, the basic word order (Subject – Verb – Object vs SOV vs VSO etc.) can be used as the basis of typology, or whether adpositions come before (prepositions) or after (postpositions) their noun phrases, or whether adjectives precede nouns or follow them. A combination of features may be used in proposing a typology.

Universals （语言）共性

In psycholinguistics, this refers to the innate features of human language that a child is assumed to be born with. In comparing the world's languages, some features are found to be common: all languages appear to have a class of verb words and a class of noun words. Sometimes, universals are better expressed as tendencies; so, for example, SOV languages (see **typology**) tend to put adjectives before nouns and to have postpositions, whereas SVO languages tend to put adjectives after nouns (as in French) and to use prepositions.

Wave model 波浪理论

The view of language development that compares language change to the effect of dropping a stone into a pond: the successive ripples (waves) become weaker, the further away they get from the centre. As stones are dropped into different places in the pond, each produces their own wave effect (i.e. changes originating among different groups of speakers), so the changes interact and languages develop accordingly. Compare **Stammbaum model.**

Applied linguistics

Applied linguistics 应用语言学

In principle, this term applies to any application of linguistics to issues involving language in the real world; in practice, applied linguistics has become synonymous with the teaching and learning of a second language, and especially English as a second/foreign language. Other significant areas of applied linguistics include: speech and language pathology and therapy; translation and interpreting; lexicography; forensic linguistics; natural language processing; educational linguistics – each of which has an entry below.

Assessment/test 评估 / 测试

In second language teaching, issues of language assessment and testing have spawned considerable research and the development of 'language testing' as a recognized subfield of applied linguistics, with many publications and its own journals. See, for example: www.le.ac.uk/education/testing/ltr.html.

Audiolingual method 听说（教学）法

Based on a behaviourist approach to language, this method viewed language learning as a matter of habit formation. Mistakes were, therefore, to be avoided and correct language reinforced. Oral presentation of language preceded the written (hence 'audio-lingual'). There was an emphasis on correct pronunciation and grammar, and on using repetition to inculcate correct language.

CALL (computer-assisted language learning)
计算机辅助语言学习

An acronym for 'computer-assisted language learning', which looks at all the possibilities of harnessing information technology to the task of teaching and learning a second/foreign language. With the increase in functionality of computer hardware, including sound and video, the applications of computer technology to the task of language learning have burgeoned. See: www.ict4lt.org.

Communicative approach 交际（教学）法

A method of teaching languages, developed in the UK in the 1960s as a reaction to the **audiolingual method**. It aimed to enable learners to use language as a means of expression in interaction, in large part by using authentic examples of language in teaching and by introducing practice activities that simulated real communication. The emphasis is on being able to communicate in real situations, rather than on correctness in pronunciation and grammar.

Communicative competence 交际能力

The notion that being a competent speaker of a language includes not only the appropriate use of grammatical features, but also the ability to be pragmatically appropriate, i.e. using language that conforms to the norms of the situational context. Introduced in the 1960s by the sociolinguist Dell Hymes, it underlies the **communicative approach** to language teaching.

Computational linguistics 计算语言学

See **natural language processing.**

Contrastive analysis 对比分析

Originating in the 1950s as a technique for comparing the language to be learnt with the learner's first language, with the aim of predicting the learning task, i.e. the contrasts between the two languages. Such a behaviourist enterprise was found to be flawed, but contrastive linguistics continued both as a contribution to understanding language learning errors (see **error analysis**) and in order to help teachers (especially of English as a foreign language) who did not share their learner's first language to understand the differences in pronunciation, grammar and vocabulary that their learners were coping with. See James (1980).

Direct method 直接（教学）法

A method of teaching foreign languages that laid great emphasis on speaking and which used only the foreign language in the classroom. The assumption underlying the direct method was that learning a second language could replicate the experience of acquiring one's first language. No explanations of grammar were to be given; grammar was to be acquired inductively; and no translation was allowed.

Eco-linguistics 生态语言学

The application of linguistics in the areas of ecology and the environment. It examines and critiques languages for anthropocentrism – the depiction of nature from a purely human perspective. More widely, it examines the 'ecology of languages', e.g. how languages interact and co-exist with each other in a defined geographical area. See the Eco-linguistics website: http://www-gewi.kfunigraz.ac.at/ed/project/ecoling/.

Educational linguistics 教育语言学

The application of linguistics to education, especially in teaching language skills and inculcating language awareness. It proposes what might be taught about language in schools, suggests curricula, advocates public examinations in English language/linguistics, and provides advice and guidance for teachers. See the website of the UK Committee for Linguistics in Education (CLIE): www.phon.ucl.ac.uk/home/dick/ec/clietop.htm.

Error analysis 偏误分析

The study of the errors made by learners of a second language, in order to understand the strategies used by second language learners and to improve second language pedagogy. Error analysis can be seen as a counterpart to **contrastive analysis**. A central text is James (1998).

Forensic linguistics 法律语言学 / 司法语言学

The application of linguistics to crime and the law. It may involve the analysis of speech samples, to assign a voice to a person; or the analysis of texts, such as witness statements or police reports, to establish their authenticity or whether they have been subsequently tampered with; or the analysis more generally of legal language in all its manifestations. An introductory textbook is Olsson (2004). See also: http://web.bham.ac.uk/forensic/index.html.

Four skills 四项（语言）技能

This term refers to the language skills of listening, speaking, reading, and writing. These may form an organizing principle in the teaching of a foreign language, as well as in school curricula for the majority language. See the national curriculum for English in England: www.curriculumonline.gov.uk/ Subjects/En/Subject.htm.

Interference （母语）干扰

In the learning of a second or subsequent language, the negative influence (language **transfer**) from the speaker's first language to the language being learned, so that they use, inappropriately, language items or structures from their first language in speaking or writing the second. Such instances of potential interference may be identified by **contrastive analysis**.

Interlanguage 中介语 / 语际语 / 过渡语

A term introduced by Larry Selinker to denote the developing second language that a learner is in the process of acquiring. It represents any intermediate language state between the start of learning and the equivalent of adult native-speaker competence. Examination of learners' interlanguages can enable teachers to understand the processes of language learning that different groups of learners may employ in acquiring a specific second language.

Language awareness 语言意识

Promoting and raising understanding of language and languages, including the teaching and learning of and about language(s). The language awareness movement aims to influence the attitudes to and teaching of language(s) in the education system. See the website for the Association of Language Awareness: www.lexically.net/ala.

Language planning and policy 语言规划与政策

The application of linguistics to decision making about language status and use at a national or regional level. Linguists may be called upon, for example, to advise governments; or they may be members of language academies; or they may proffer advice, solicited or unsolicited, through national organizations such as the British Association for Applied Linguistics (www.baal.org.uk).

Lexicography 词典学

The application of linguistics to the writing of dictionaries, taking the outputs of linguistic description and using them to construct entries for words and other lexical items in dictionaries. Lexicography, however, has a long history that is independent of the development of modern linguistics, which has, though, increased its influence since the 1960s. Lexicography is also the academic subject that studies dictionaries and associated reference books. See Hartmann & James (2001).

Literacy 读写能力

The acquisition of the skills of reading and writing (see **four skills**). **Educational linguistics** has an input to literacy, along with psychology, pedagogy and neuro-science, especially in explaining grapheme-phoneme correspondences, different orthographies and scripts, as well as language structure more generally, as this is relevant to the processes of reading and writing.

LSP (language for special purposes) 专用语言

An acronym for 'language for special purposes', which also encompasses ESP (English for Special Purposes) and EAP (English for Academic Purposes). LSP contributes to second language learning and teaching where students need to learn a language for a specific purpose, e.g. business communication, studying engineering, working as a hospital doctor.

Minority rights 少数族群权利

In the context of **language planning and policy**, linguistics can be applied to the problems of speech communities that speak a minority language, e.g. Catalan in Spain, or to the situation of languages that are threatened with extinction. The European Bureau for Lesser Used Languages monitors and champions minority languages in Europe (see www.eblul.org). More widely, the Foundation for Endangered Languages (www.ogmios.org) promotes awareness of languages that are under threat.

Motivation 动机　　attitude 态度

These have been found to be important factors in the successful learning of a second language, and there has been much research devoted to them. A distinction is often drawn between 'instrumental' motivation, where a second language is learned because it can achieve something for the learner, e.g. a better job, access to higher education, and 'integrative' motivation, where a second language is learned because the learner wishes to participate in the society and culture of the language's speakers. The classic text is Gardner & Lambert (1972).

Natural language processing 自然语言处理

The application of linguistics to the problems of representing language in computer systems and of human-computer interaction. A range of problems, from synthesizing speech to developing sophisticated grammar and style checkers to machine translation, is tackled by NLP researchers. NLP is often regarded as a sub-discipline of Artificial Intelligence (AI), but is perhaps more sensibly regarded as a branch of computational linguistics. See the website of the Association for Computational Linguistics: www.aclweb.org.

Speech and language pathology 言语和语言病理学

The application of linguistics to the study and treatment of communication impairments in children and of those acquired by adults as a result of brain damage, e.g. following a stroke (see **aphasia** in the Psycholinguistics section). Linguistics is a crucial subject studied by those training to be speech and language therapists. In the UK, the profession is represented by the Royal College of Speech and Language Therapists (www.rcslt.org).

Stylistics 文体学

The application of linguistics to the study of all genres of literature, and especially to the study of authorial style. This is a vast area of research; for more details see the separate section on Stylistics.

Transfer （母语）迁移

A term in **contrastive analysis** to refer to the use of an element from a learner's first language in their developing second language (**interlanguage**). Transfer may be positive, if the second language shares the feature transferred from the first; but more often it is negative, if the feature is realized partly or wholly differently in the second language.

Translation 笔译   interpreting 口译

The application of linguistics to the process of rendering a text from one language into another, or of providing a simultaneous (or consecutive) translation of speech. Linguistics can provide insight not only into the structures of the source and target languages, but also into issues relating to discourse and text types, sociolinguistic norms, pragmatics, and so on. The use of computers in translation is a major field in **natural language processing**.

Stylistics

Style 风格

The identifying linguistic features of a text (the style of *Pride and Prejudice*), or of a text type/genre (an expository style, journalistic style, the style of the Old English epic poem), or of an author (Jane Austen's style), or of a text using a particular style (ironic style, the style of parody). The linguistic features that constitute a style may be phonological (e.g. in poetry), grammatical, lexical, or some combination of these.

Stylistics 文体学

The study of style, especially of literature (literary stylistics), but in principle of any type of text (e.g. advertising, political speeches, obituaries). Using the techniques of descriptive linguistics and the insights of one or more theoretical linguistic models, a stylistician studies the language of their chosen text(s) with the aim of discovering the linguistic features that mark the text(s) as different from other types of text or other authors. The results of a stylistic analysis may contribute to the interpretation of the text(s) within literary criticism, or from a critical linguistics perspective, or simply as a contribution to this sub-discipline of linguistics. For a more detailed glossary, see Wales (2001).

Alliteration 头韵

The repetition of a consonant at the beginning of two or more successive words, e.g. <u>little Lawrence was laid low</u>. Alliteration is an important feature that characterizes the style of Old English poetry, e.g. the following line from *Beowulf*: swa sceal geong guma gode gewyrcean. Compare **assonance**.

Anacoluthon 错格 / 破格

A stylistic effect involving beginning and ending a sentence with discordant grammar, i.e. beginning with one sentence construction, but not following it through to its expected conclusion, e.g. 'It's amazing that he … why didn't he complain?' Compare **false start** in the Discourse & Text Analysis section.

Assonance 谐元韵 / 半谐韵

The repetition of a vowel sound in successive words for stylistic effect, usually in poetry, e.g. <u>my late great mate</u>. Compare **alliteration**.

Consonance 辅音韵

The repetition of a final consonant, usually with a different preceding vowel, e.g. 'n' in <u>seven lean men</u>. When used at the end of lines in poetry, it is called a 'half-rhyme'. Compare **alliteration**, **assonance**.

Diction 措词 / 措辞

This refers to an author's choice of words. In general terms, an author's diction may be characteristic of them and identify their style; they may be said, for example, to have a 'formal' or 'informal' diction. Within a work of fiction, an author may give each character a different diction, as part of their characterization.

Direct speech 直接引语   indirect speech 间接引语

Direct speech quotes what a character says or thinks, e.g. 'She said, "I won't see him tomorrow". Indirect speech is the narrator's reporting of what a character says, e.g. 'She said that she would not see him the next day', resulting in various changes, such as first person pronoun (I) to third person (she), tense from present (won't see) to past (would not see). Compare **free indirect speech**.

Effect 效果

The result of the conscious manipulation of linguistic features – phonological, grammatical or lexical – for stylistic purposes. For example, fronting a syntactic object may create a stylistic effect: 'The names of his wife and children he couldn't remember any more' instead of 'He couldn't remember the names of his wife and children any more'.

Eye rhyme 眼韵/目韵/视韵/视觉韵

The letters of two words match, but the pronunciations do not, e.g. bound and wound; so it is a rhyme to the reader's eye, but not to the ear.

Field 语场　　tenor 语旨　　mode 语式

Categories proposed by Michael Halliday to account for the stylistic features of texts and discourses. 'Field' refers to the subject matter of the text, what the text is about. 'Tenor' refers to the participants who are involved in giving and receiving the text, and their role relationships. 'Mode' refers to how the text is communicated, primarily whether it is spoken or written. All of these involve linguistic choices that have an impact on the style of a text or discourse. See Halliday (1973).

Foot 音步

In poetry, a sequence of stressed and unstressed syllables that is repeated to form a **metre**. For example, an iambic foot consists of unstressed + stressed syllables, a dactylic foot of stressed + unstressed + unstressed.

Foregrounding 前景化

A term taken from art criticism to refer to the use of stylistic devices to give prominence to certain aspects of a text. At its simplest, a word or phrase could be foregrounded by printing it in larger or bold type, or by underlining it. Foregrounding is more usually indicated in text by grammatical, lexical or semantic 'deviance', or by 'parallelism'. An example of deviance would be in the following line from an E. E. Cummings poem: 'anyone lived in a pretty how town', where anyone is used as a kind of proper name, and the adverb how is used as an adjective. Here is an example of parallelism of structure from Psalm 23: 'he leads me beside quiet waters … he guides me in paths of righteousness'.

Free indirect speech (or style) 自由间接引语

A technique of depicting a character's speech or thoughts in the third person, as if from their **point of view**, so that narrator's and character's views become intermingled. For example, in 'He would go and call on her tomorrow', the form of the verb (would go and call on) derives from indirect speech, but the adverb (tomorrow) is more akin to direct speech. Compare **direct/indirect speech**.

Genre 体裁

A term used to refer to different types of (literary) text, each of which is characterized by a broad set of stylistic features. A basic division is made, among literary texts, into the genres of poetry, drama, and prose. Within each of these, sub-genres, and further sub-divisions, are usually recognized. For example, poetry is divided into 'epic' and 'lyric', drama into 'tragedy' and 'comedy', prose into 'novel', 'short story' and 'essay', and so on. Genre is a rather vague term and is applied in a variety of ways. See also the entry for **genre** in the Discourse and Text Analysis section.

Hyperbole 夸张

Overstatement or exaggeration, made for stylistic **effect**, e.g. if you say 'I've got a million things to do'. Compare **litotes**.

Irony 反语 / 讽刺

In language, irony involves using words that mean something close to the opposite of their normal denotation, e.g. saying 'That's good' when the opposite is obviously the case.

Litotes 曲言 / 间接肯定

Understatement, especially by using a negative with ironic effect, e.g. 'They are not the most co-operative of people', meaning that they are 'very uncooperative'. Compare **hyperbole**.

Metaphor 隐喻

The transference of meaning from one word/concept to another. For example, if someone says 'I'm a night owl', the meaning of 'active and awake at night', which is associated with owls, is transferred to the speaker. The two parts of the metaphorical relationship have been termed 'tenor' or 'target' and 'vehicle' or 'source', I and owl respectively in the example above. Compare **simile**. See also the entry for **metaphor** in the Semantics and Pragmatics section.

Metonymy 转喻 / 借喻 / 借代

The use of a part or a feature of something to refer to the whole, e.g. crown for the monarchy, dish for a course in a meal, the Kremlin for the Russian government.

Metre 韵律 / 格律

The rhythmical patterns in poetry. A metre consists of a sequence of metrical **feet**. Four metres are normally identified in the description of English poetry: iambic (unstressed + stressed syllable), anapaestic (two unstressed + stressed), trochaic (stressed + unstressed), dactylic (stressed + two unstressed). A metre with five feet is called a 'pentameter', with six feet a 'hexameter'.

Narrative 叙事体 / 记叙文

A text type that is characterized by actions/events that are determined by their location in time. Narratives are studied by the stylistics subdiscipline of 'narratology'. Of particular interest is the role of the narrator, **point of view**, characterization, plot structure, etc. An introductory text is Toolan (2001).

Onomatopoeia 拟声

A phonological stylistic feature, where the sound (pronunciation) of a word in some way reflects the word's denotation. For example, cuckoo resembles the call of this bird, didgeridoo is imitative of the sound produced by this Australian Aboriginal musical instrument. Edgar Allan Poe's poem 'The Bells' makes extensive use of onomatopoeia.

Parody 仿拟

The imitation of a work of literature, or the style of an author or genre, usually for humorous or polemical purposes. For example, Pope's poem 'The Rape of the Lock' is a parody of heroic epic poems, as it applies this poetic form to the telling of a trivial incident.

Point of view 叙事角度 / 视角

In **narrative** texts, the 'narrator' tells the story from their perspective or 'point of view'. The point of view in a story may change as the author has different narrators tell it from their particular angle. In general terms, narratives may be told from a 'first person' point of view, or from a 'third person' point of view. A narrator may be 'external' to the story ('nonfocalized' point of view), or 'internal' to the story ('focalized' point of view).

Reception theory 接受理论

An approach to stylistics and literary reception that focuses on the reader. It proposes that reading is an act of interpretation, to which the reader brings their life experience; so that there is no one 'reading' of a text, but rather an act of negotiation in a relationship between a text and its reader(s). Communities of readers with similar backgrounds may have readings that coincide to a greater or lesser extent.

Register 语域

A term that is variously used in different sub-disciplines of linguistics. In stylistics, register refers to a text variety (**genre**) from the perspective of its use or setting. For some, register is a matter of formality, ranging from 'very formal' (frozen) to 'very informal' (casual). For others, where the concentration is on choice of vocabulary, it correlates to 'jargon'; so 'officialese' or 'legalese' would be classed as registers.

Rhyme 韵脚 / 尾韵 / 押韵

Two words rhyme when the sound (pronunciation) of their endings is identical, e.g. <u>fall</u>, <u>tall</u>; <u>care</u>, <u>fair</u>. In a 'masculine' rhyme, the final syllable is stressed, e.g. <u>debate</u>, <u>inflate</u>. In a 'feminine' rhyme the stress falls on the penultimate syllable, e.g. <u>maker</u>, <u>taker</u>.

Scheme 韵式

In stylistics, this term applies to **metre** or **rhyme**. A metrical scheme is one employed by a poet in a particular composition to structure the rhythmical **effect**s of the text. It may follow one of the classical metrical patterns, e.g. iambic pentameter, or it may be a variation on this. A rhyme scheme describes the pattern of rhyming in a stanza; for example, Shakespearian sonnets usually have the pattern a-b-a-b c-d-c-d e-f-e-f g-g, i.e. the first line rhymes with the third, and so on.

Simile 明喻

The characterization of a person or thing by comparison with something else, usually by means of the words <u>like</u> or <u>as</u>; for example, in the first line of Robert Burns' poem, 'My love is like a red, red rose', or Wordsworth's 'I wandered lonely as a cloud'. Compare: **metaphor**.

Stylometry 计算文体学 / 计量文体学 / 计量风格学

The stylistic comparison of texts, often to establish disputed authorship, e.g. of some works attributed to Shakespeare; in recent times stylometry has used computational methods and applied sophisticated statistical analysis to such investigations. Many such studies have been reported in the journal *Literary and Linguistic Computing* (Oxford University Press).

Synecdoche 提喻

An expression in which a part stands for the whole or an individual for a class of things, or material for the things made from it; e.g. in 'The crown owns this land', <u>the crown</u> is used to stand for the monarch (compare **metonymy**); in 'the sound of leather on willow', <u>leather</u> stands for a cricket ball, and <u>willow</u> for a cricket bat – the materials from which they are made. The reverse, where the whole stands for a part, may also apply, e.g. when a police officer is referred to as <u>the law</u>.

Trope 修辞格

A rhetorical device involving a play on words, such as **metonymy**, e.g. using <u>Whitehall</u> to denote the British Civil Service, or **synecdoche**, or **metaphor**. In literary criticism, trope has another use: a familiar symbol or theme often found in a particular **genre**, e.g. the *femme fatale* in drama.

Zeugma 轭式修辞法 / 轭式搭配

A **trope** involving the joining together (*zeugma* is Greek for 'yoke') of two or more constructions, usually with a common verb, e.g. 'Prudence dictates caution, exuberance spontaneity'. A particular kind of zeugma is syllepsis, in which two incongruous nouns are objects of the same verb, e.g. 'He stole her heart and her bicycle'.

Corpus linguistics

Corpus 语料库

Plural **corpora**; a collection of texts, or text samples, or transcribed speech, or a combination of these, used for the purposes of linguistic analysis and description. An early corpus was the Survey of English Usage, begun in 1959 and directed by Randolph Quirk at University College London; the work on the Survey continues (see www.ucl.ac.uk/english-usage). Originally a paper-based corpus, the SEU has now been computerized. Since the first computer corpus (the Brown Corpus, put together by Nelson Francis and Henry Kučera at Brown University in the USA in the 1960s), corpora are understood to be stored electronically. A survey of corpora can be found at: bowland-files.lancs.ac.uk/corplang/cbls/corpora.asp.

Corpus linguistics 语料库语言学

An empirical method of linguistic analysis and description that uses a **corpus** as its primary data and starting point. This method is in contrast to introspective linguistics (sometimes called 'armchair' linguistics), where the linguist describes a language on the basis of their own knowledge and speculates about the nature of language on this basis. See the website 'Text Corpora and Corpus Linguistics': www.athel.com/corpus.html and devoted.to/corpora. An introductory textbook is

McEnery & Wilson (2001).

Annotation 标注／标码

Additional information accompanying a text in a **corpus**. The information may be part of the text's **header**, relating, for example, to its provenance; or it may be inserted in the text itself as a **tag** or **parse**. Annotation usually conforms to the **TEI** guidelines. Compare **markup**.

Balanced corpus 平衡语料库

A corpus whose composition represents different genres of text in equal or appropriate proportions. Some corpora are composed exclusively of written material, e.g. the Brown corpus (see www.essex.ac.uk/w3c/corpus_ling/content/corpora/list/private/brown/brown.html) and its British counterpart, **LOB**. Where a corpus has a spoken element, it is often a small percentage of the corpus material, e.g. 10% of the **British National Corpus**. An attempt to balance spoken and written material from different genres is made by the **ICE** project (see www.ucl.ac.uk/english-usage/ice/).

Bank of English 柯林斯英语语料库

A large **monitor corpus** (latest release 450 million words and growing), owned by University of Birmingham, UK and HarperCollins Publishers. It was originally set up for the COBUILD project, which produced the COBUILD Dictionary and associated materials for foreign learners of English. It continues to be maintained at Birmingham University and can be accessed by scholars (see www.titania.bham.ac.uk). A 56-million-word subset of the BoE can be searched online, at www.collins.co.uk/Corpus/CorpusSearch. aspx.

British National Corpus 英国国家语料库

A 100-million-word **balanced corpus**, compiled in the early 1990s by a consortium of publishers and universities, and now managed at the University of Oxford (see www.natcorp.ox.ac.uk). The corpus can be searched online at: thetis.bl.uk/lookup.html, but only a limited output is given. It is also accessible at the VIEW website: view.byu.edu. A counterpart American National Corpus is in the process of construction (see www. americannationalcorpus.org).

Collocate 搭配

A word that is found to occur regularly within a defined **span** of a **node** word; the collocate and the node form a 'collocation', which is a feature of their meaning (see Semantics and Pragmatics section). Using a large corpus is a reliable way of finding out about collocation.

Computational linguistics 计算语言学

The application of computer science to the processing of natural language, including the development of software for purposes such as automatic grammatical and lexical analysis, machine translation, knowledge representation, speech analysis and synthesis. It intersects with corpus linguistics in areas such as **tagging** and **parsing**.

Concordance 检索行 / 索引行

A list of all the occurrences of a (key) word in a corpus, together with a specified amount of co-text on either side of the keyword, i.e. in **KWIC** format. A concordance is produced by a piece of concordancing software, e.g. MonoConc (www.monoconc.com), WordSmith Tools (www.lexically.net/wordsmith/index.html). Concordancing software is the basic tool of corpus linguists.

Encoding 编码

The preparation of a text in a specified format for inclusion in a corpus, including any **annotation** and **markup**. The emphasis is on the standardization of encoding formats (e.g. **TEI**) and the consequent reusability of corpora.

Frequency 频率

The number of times an item occurs in a corpus. Corpus linguistics has made possible reliable investigations into the frequencies of words and other language elements (e.g. I shall vs I will). Frequency lists for the **British National Corpus** can be found at: www. comp.lancs.ac.uk/ucrel/ bncfreq/; and for the **Oxford English Corpus** at: www.askoxford.com/ oec/mainpage/oec02/?view = uk.

Hapax legomenon 孤频词 / 一次词

Plural legomena, from Greek, 'something said once'; a word that has a single occurrence in a corpus.

Header 文本头 / 标头

An **annotation** at the beginning of a text in a corpus, giving information such as where the text or sample came from, the author or speaker, the date of publication or utterance, the genre to which it is assigned, its size, and so on. Besides giving background information to the text, such information properly encoded can be used for sorting or selection, when a researcher is investigating just texts from a particular genre, for example.

Historical corpus 历时语料库

A corpus of texts from across the history of a language, e.g. from Old English to Modern English. The representative historical corpus for English is the 1.6-million-word Helsinki Corpus, with texts from Old English to around 1700 (see khnt.hit.uib.no/icame/manuals/HC/ INDEX.HTM). This is being supplemented by the Archer Corpus, with texts from 1650 to 1990.

ICAME (International Computer Archive of Modern and Medieval English)
国际现代及中古英语计算机档案协会

The International Computer Archive of Modern and Medieval English, based at the University of Bergen, Norway. It is a repository for many corpora of English, both contemporary and historical; it also holds a regular conference and publishes a journal. See http://nora.hd.uib.no/whatis.html.

International Corpus of English
国际英语语料库 / 英语国际语料库

Known as ICE and directed from University College London by Gerald Nelson. It aims to compile 15 one-million-word corpora of national and regional varieties of English from around the world, according to a common design and using spoken and written material from after 1989. Details at: www.ucl.ac.uk/english-usage/ice/index.htm.

KWIC (key word in context) （语境中的）关键词索引

An acronym for 'key word in context'; it is the usual format in which a **concordance** is presented, with the keyword in the centre of the page and the same amount of co-text either side, e.g.

> Boris's mother would call him **graceful**. The Becker game is founded on power
> their ugly stamp on it. A **graceful** drive led to a double flight of steps
> brand new uniform, beside a **graceful** girl who was filling her water-jar from a

Lemmatization 词形归并 / 词形还原

In analysing a corpus, different inflectional forms of a word are assigned to their appropriate lemma (base form), e.g. <u>shows</u>, <u>showing</u>, <u>showed</u>, <u>shown</u> are all treated as forms of the lemma <u>show</u> and not as separate words. Lemmatization is more difficult to automate when there are irregular forms to account for, e.g. <u>goes</u>, <u>going</u>, <u>went</u>, <u>gone</u> as forms of the lemma go. Whether lemmatization has taken place or not can be significant when calculating **frequency** statistics.

LOB (Lancaster-Oslo/Bergen corpus)
兰卡斯特—奥斯陆／卑尔根语料库

An acronym for the Lancaster-Oslo/Bergen corpus, the one-million-word British counterpart to the American Brown corpus, with 500 text samples of 2,000 words each from a range of genres in material published in 1961. The LOB corpus was composed in the 1970s, initially at the University of Lancaster under the direction of Geoffrey Leech, and then at the University of Oslo under the direction of Stig Johansson. Full details can be found at: khnt.hit.uib.no/icame/manuals/lob/INDEX.HTM.

Markup 标注／标码
Another term for **annotation**. Compare **SGML**.

Monitor corpus （动态）监察语料库

An open-ended corpus, to which a certain amount of text is regularly added, with the aim of 'monitoring' changes and developments in the language, and especially to identify new words as they are coined and come into use. The **Bank of English** is intended to be a monitor corpus.

Node 节点

The word whose **collocate**s are being sought within a defined **span**, e.g. graceful in the example at **KWIC**.

Oxford English Corpus 牛津英语语料库

A one-billion-word corpus, compiled by the Oxford University Press dictionary department from material found on the internet. It is used for lexicographic purposes, and researchers have discovered some interesting **frequency** data, e.g. the most common 100 words account for about half of all text, and the most frequent 1000 for about three-quarters of all text. (See: www. askoxford.com/oec/?view = uk, or follow the link from the AskOxford homepage: www.askoxford.com.)

Parallel corpus 平行语料库

A corpus comprising texts from two or more languages that are usually translations of each other. Alternatively, a parallel corpus may contain texts in two languages from the same genre or text type, e.g. legal texts, or government documents. Parallel corpora have been used in developing machine-assisted translation.

Parsed corpus 句法标注语料库

A corpus that has been subject to **parsing**, either automatically or manually. The British component of the **International Corpus of English** has been released in a parsed version (see: www.ucl.ac.uk/english-usage/projects/ice-gb/index.htm). A parsed corpus allows investigations of the corpus by searching on the parse **tags**, thus enabling more sophisticated grammatical research to be undertaken. Compare **tagged corpus**.

Parsing 句法标注/句法解析

The process of assigning a grammatical analysis, either automatically using software written for the purpose, or manually, to the sentences in a corpus. Usually an automatic parse requires some pre- and post-editing.

Representative corpus 代表性语料库/平衡语料库

Another term for **balanced corpus**, with the emphasis on having the texts in the corpus 'representative' of the state of the language at the specified time period.

Sample corpus 样本语料库   full-text corpus 全文语料库

A sample corpus, such as **LOB**, is composed of text extracts (2000-word samples in the case of LOB), whereas a full-text corpus, such as the **Bank of English**, is composed of whole texts (e.g. a complete magazine or a whole novel).

SGML (standard generalized markup language) 标准通用标注语言

An acronym for 'standard generalized markup language', an internationally recognized set of **annotation**s and **tag**s for use when digitizing texts, whether for corpus purposes or not. The **TEI** used SGML in their guidelines. SGML has now been largely superseded by XML, a restricted version of SGML (see www.xml.com).

Span 跨距

The number of words to the left and right of a **node** within which **collocate**s of the node are searched for. A span of up to five words is usually chosen for this purpose.

Tag 赋码

A label added to a word to indicate its part-of-speech (word class) or other grammatical designation. Tags usually make fine distinctions among the members of a word class, e.g. between proper and common nouns, comparative and superlative adjectives.

Tagged corpus 词性标注语料库

A corpus that has been furnished with part-of-speech **tag**s. A tagged corpus allows researchers to look for words by tag, thus permitting more sophisticated grammatical analyses than is possible with a 'plain' text. Compare **parsed corpus**.

Tagset （词性）标注集 / 赋码集

The set of **tags** employed in a specific **tagged corpus**. For example, see www.comp.lancs.ac.uk/ucrel/clawsl tags.html for the tagset used for **LOB**.

TEI (text encoding initiative)
文本编码计划 / 文本编码倡议

An acronym for the Text Encoding Initiative, an international undertaking to provide a set of standardized Guidelines for scholars intending to digitize texts. Based on **SGML**, the TEI Guidelines were originally published in 1994 and have been used widely in text digitization. The TEI's website is at: www.tei-c.org.

Token 形符

An instance of a word in a corpus; counting the tokens in a corpus means counting the running words, as in a word processor's 'word count'; spaces constitute the boundaries of tokens. Compare **type**.

Treebank 树图数据库 / 树图语料库

A corpus that has undergone **parsing**, so that its sentences are annotated with syntactic structures (trees).

Type 类符

Each 'different' word in a corpus; for example, all the occurrences (**token**s) of <u>and</u> in a corpus constitute a single 'type'; the count of types is a count of the number of different words that a corpus contains. **Lemmatization** is a further stage in grouping words together.

Type/token ratio 类符 / 形符比

The number of **types** in a corpus divided by the number of **tokens**. This measure gives an indication of the 'lexical density' of a text, and it has been used as a factor in calculating 'readability' scores. The nearer the type/token ratio is to 1, the more lexically dense the text is; a score of 1 means that every word is different.

Schools of linguistics

Theories and models 理论与模型

When studying any natural phenomena, whether in the natural world or in human behaviour, scholars aim to use methods that are rigorous and objective, and they work within a framework that defines the basic terms and provides a model or theory about the phenomena. Investigations will often test the hypotheses generated by the theory, or serve to make the theory more accurate and serviceable. Modern linguistics, as a relatively young (social) science, has seen a plethora of models and theories proposed over the last century. We cannot include them all, so the following explains the key terms in the most influential theories. We first present the theories briefly and then introduce the key terms for each. For a review of modern linguistics, see Joseph *et al.* (2001).

Structuralism 结构主义

The term given to the model proposed by the acknowledged founder of modern linguistics, Ferdinand de Saussure (1857-1913), whose lectures, gathered together by two of his students after his death and published as *Cours de Linguistique Générale* (1916), have been enormously influential for linguistics generally. The term is also used for the approach to linguistics in the USA that followed from the work of Leonard Bloomfield (1887-1949), encapsulated in his book *Language* (1933), and based on a strictly behaviourist and empiricist methodology.

Systemic-functional linguistics 系统功能语言学

Building on the work of the British linguist J. R. Firth (1890-1960), this model has been developed principally by M. A. K. Halliday (1925-). It is a functional model, in that it approaches language as a social phenomenon and sees language as shaped by the uses to which speakers put it. See Halliday & Matthiessen (2004), Eggins (2004).

Transformational generative grammar 转换生成语法

The models of linguistics based on the work of Noam Chomsky (1928-), beginning with his seminal work *Syntactic Structures* (1957), in which the notion of 'transformations' was proposed, and elaborated in *Aspects of the Theory of Syntax* (1965) and subsequent work. There has been considerable development in Chomsky's ideas over the years, though his view of language as a psychological/biological phenomenon has remained constant, as has his view of a grammar (i.e. model of language) as a mechanism that should generate 'all and only' the sentences of a language. See Smith (1999).

Dependency grammar 依存语法

Beginning with the work of the French linguist Lucien Tesnière (1893-1954) in his work *Esquisse d'une syntaxe structurale* (1953), the description of syntactic structure in terms of dependencies between units has developed especially in Germany with the notion of 'Valenz' (valency), e.g. in the work of Gerhard Helbig in the context of German as a foreign language, and in the work of Rudolf Emons in relation to English. See Fischer (2003). Richard (Dick) Hudson's 'Word Grammar' is an example of a dependency grammar in the British context; see Hudson (2007) for the latest version.

Cognitive linguistics 认知语言学

A quite recent and developing model of language with its beginnings in the 1970s, which goes back to the question of how we 'make meaning'. It draws inspiration from cognitive psychology and views language processes as instances of more general cognitive processes; it suggests that understanding language requires far more than just linguistic processing. One of the pioneers is Ronald Langacker (1942-), who formulated his ideas in the two volumes of *Foundations of Cognitive Grammar* (1987, 1991). For a survey of the model, see Croft & Cruse (2004).

Structuralism (Saussure) 结构主义（索绪尔）

Diachronic 历时的   synchronic 共时的

The distinction made by Saussure between studying language from the historical perspective, i.e. diachronically, which had dominated linguistic research in the nineteenth century, and studying a language at a particular point in time, especially the contemporary language, i.e. synchronically, which was championed by Saussure.

Langue 语言   parole 言语

The distinction between language as a system (langue), which is the property of a speech community, and language as the utterances of individuals (parole). The proper study for the synchronic linguist is 'langue', the shared social entity. A third related term used by Saussure was 'langage', which denoted the language faculty in human beings.

Sign 符号   signifier 能指/意符   signified 所指/意指

'Langue' is a system of signs, and a sign is the relationship between a signified (concept) and a signifier (an acoustic or graphical form). The relation between a signifier and its signified is arbitrary, as evidenced by different words in different languages for the same concept. Saussure compared the system of signs to a game of chess: just as the addition or loss of a chess piece alters the state of the game, so the addition or loss of a sign changes the language system.

Syntagmatic （横）组合（关系）
paradigmatic （纵）聚合（关系）

The two axes on which signs relate to each other. The paradigmatic axis is the vertical one, on which signs are in a relationship of contrast or similarity with each other, representing an axis of choice for any place in structure. The syntagmatic axis is the horizontal one, on which signs are in a relationship of combination with each other (e.g. in phrases and sentences).

Structuralism (Bloomfield) 结构主义（布龙菲尔德）

Discovery procedures 发现程序

In this strictly empiricist model, linguists had to start from the data of language (what people say and write), without any theoretical preconceptions. The model formulated a set of discovery procedures to guide the linguist in their approaches to a set of language data. For example, the phonemes of the language had to be established first, and only then the morphemes, words and larger units.

Distribution 分布

The places in structure where a linguistic item regularly occurs. Observing and charting the distribution of items was a necessary step towards grouping items into **form class**es. If items were in 'complementary distribution', then they could be variants of the same class. This was an important criterion for establishing the phonemes of a language; for example, in English the unaspirated [p] after /s/ in <u>spin</u> and the aspirated [pʰ] in <u>pin</u> are variants of the phoneme /p/ on the basis that they are in complementary distribution.

Form class 形类／形式类

A set of items (morphemes, words, phrases, etc.) established on the basis of their common distribution in structure. For example, the class of 'adjectives' includes those words that have the following distribution: between a/the and a noun (the red apple); after the verb be in the **frame** 'the N is __' (the apple is red).

Frame 框架

A structure for testing the **distribution** of linguistic items. A frame contains an empty slot, and the items entering that slot are candidates for a **form class**. For example, in the frame 'the N __ the N', the class of transitive verbs could be expected to occur, or alternatively the class of prepositions.

Immediate constituent analysis 直接成分分析法

The technique for analysing the syntax of sentences into their 'immediate constituents'. The assumption was that the analysis proceeded by a series of binary steps: an initial division of a sentence into two, then the division of those immediate constituents into two, and so on.

Taxonomy 分类法

Successors to Bloomfieldian structuralism accused it of being interested only in taxonomy, i.e. the grouping of linguistic items into classes. This may indeed have been the main thrust of the Bloomfieldian approach, but taxonomy is an important part of the study of any natural phenomena, and it continues to be relevant to the study of language.

Systemic-functional linguistics 系统功能语言学

Action 行动

A type of **process**, in which an actor **participant** instigates a change in a state of affairs, e.g. <u>smile</u>, <u>send</u>, <u>report</u>. Compare **mental process**, **relation**.

Circumstance 环境

The attendant situation to a **process**, such as the time it took place, its location, the manner in which it happened, and so on. Compare **participant**.

Function 功能

The communicative purpose of a **text** or aspect of a text. Three functions are identified: **ideational**, **interpersonal**, **textual**.

Ideational 概念（功能）

One of the three **function**s that a **text** may have, relating to the subject matter or content of the piece of language. Compare **interpersonal**, **textual**.

Interpersonal 人际（功能）

The aspects of the **function** of a **text** that are pertinent to the relationship between the speaker/writer and the hearer/reader. For example, the 'mood' **system** is an interpersonal aspect, including the choice between 'interrogative' (asking a question or making a request) and 'declarative' (making a statement), since this reflects the relationship between the roles of speaker and hearer.

Mental process 心理过程

A type of **process**, in which an experiencer **participant** engages in thought, emotion and the like, e.g. <u>consider</u>, <u>dream</u>, <u>want</u>. Compare

KEY TERMS IN LINGUISTICS

action, relation.

Mood 语气

A **system** of the **interpersonal** function of a **text**, including the choice between 'declarative', 'interrogative', 'imperative', etc., reflecting the role that a speaker/writer assumes in relation to the hearer/reader.

Participant 参与者

An entity (person, thing, idea, etc.) involved in a **process**. In the **action** process 'The old man bought his granddaughter a new bicycle', the participants are <u>man</u> (actor), <u>granddaughter</u> (beneficiary), <u>bicycle</u> (goal).

Process 过程

What a clause is about and the **participants** are involved in. Three types of process are recognized: **action, mental process, relation.**

Relation 关系（过程）

A type of **process**, in which either one **participant** is an 'attributive' of another or one participant is 'equative' of another. For example, in 'Your mother is a brilliant cook', <u>a brilliant cook</u> is attributive of <u>your mother</u>; in 'My sister is the manager', <u>the manager</u> is equative of <u>my sister</u> (their roles are in principle reversible, i.e. 'The manager is my sister'). Compare **action, mental process.**

Rheme 述位

From the perspective of communicative function, the part of a clause that says something about the **theme**.

System 系统

A set of choices relating to one of the **function**s of a clause or **text**, e.g. the system of **mood** in the **interpersonal** function, or the system of **transitivity** in the **ideational** function. System choices interrelate to realize the syntactic and morphological features of a piece of text, i.e. the grammar of a text is the result of the choices made from the relevant systems.

Text 语篇 / 篇章

The term used for the linguistic unit that is larger than a sentence, including both spoken discourse and written text.

Textual 语篇（功能）

The aspects of the **function** of a **text** that relate to the construction of the text, and which identify it as a text rather than as a non-text. Such aspects include, for example, cohesion, such as the use of linking adverbs like <u>however</u> or <u>therefore</u>.

Theme 主位

Usually the opening element of a clause, announcing the topic of the clause; it is followed by the **rheme**, which says something new about the theme. The theme is normally 'given' information (i.e. has been mentioned before in the text), and the rheme is 'new' information.

Transitivity 及物性

A core **system** associated with the **ideational** function of a text, providing choices in respect of the type of **process** and the associated **participants** in the clause.

Transformational-generative grammar (TGG) 转换生成语法

Competence 语言能力　　performance 语言运用

Competence is the language system stored in a speaker's head, and, according to Chomsky, the proper object of linguistics; performance is the speech and writing that language users produce, and which may contain all kinds of 'mistakes'. There is a parallel with Saussure's **langue/parole** distinction, but it is not the same; Saussure's 'langue' is a social phenomenon, not a psychological one like competence.

Deep structure 深层结构

Also known in later versions of the theory as 'D-structure'; the underlying syntactic representation of a sentence before any **transformation**s have applied. Compare **surface structure**.

Government and binding 管辖与约束

A development of Chomsky's theory, first presented in *Lectures on Government and Binding* (1981), which involves four levels of 'representation' (D-structure, S-structure, Phonological Form, Logical Form) and a series of constraints.

Kernel sentence 核心句

In the early version of TGG, a basic clause, which could be combined, using appropriate **transformation**s, with other kernel sentences to form complex sentences.

Lexicon 词库

The component of the grammar containing the lexical items of a language and rules for word formation; the exact nature of the lexicon varies between versions of the theory.

Logical form 逻辑式

The term given to the semantic representation component of the grammar in later versions, e.g. **government and binding**, i.e. a representation of the meaning of a sentence.

Marker 标记

In the deep/underlying structure, indicating that an appropriate

transformation needs to operate, e.g. 'neg' to trigger a 'negative' transformation, or 'Qu' to trigger an 'interrogative' one.

Minimalist program 最简方案

A recent (1990s) development of Chomsky's theory, as in his book *The Minimalist Program* (1995), concentrating on economy in the derivation of sentences and in the representations required by the grammar. The notions of 'deep' and 'surface' structure have been jettisoned.

Movement rule 移动规则

A type of **transformation**, which moves an item from one part of a structure to another, as when the 'passive' transformation moves a syntactic object into subject position. In later versions of the theory, e.g. **government and binding**, movement rules are the only type of transformation that is permitted.

Phonological rules 音系规则 / 音位规则

The component of the grammar that specifies the pronunciation of the **surface structure** of a sentence.

Phrase structure rules 短语结构规则

The component of the grammar that generates the **deep structure** of a sentence.

Principles and parameters 原则和参数

The view, proposed by Chomsky in the early 1990s, that all languages share some basic syntactic features, the principles, which are part of 'universal grammar'; and that languages have other features that are individual, but within certain constraints – the parameters.

Projection principle 投射原则 / 映射原则

A constraint which stipulates that the properties of a lexical item must be preserved in all the stages of the generation of a phrase structure. For example, if it is a property of a verb that it requires a syntactic object, this must be associated at all times with that lexical item.

Selection rule 选择规则

This specifies for a particular item the restrictions on the choice of other items that can co-occur with it. For example, the verb <u>last</u> usually has an expression of 'extent of time' as syntactic object ('The film lasted two hours').

Semantic interpretation 语义解释

Later known as **logical form**; the representation of the meaning of a sentence, in early versions of the theory considered to be a matter of 'interpretation' of the **deep structure** of a sentence.

Subcategorization 子语类化 / 次范畴化

The specification for a lexical item of the syntactic elements that co-occur with it. For example, the verb <u>fell</u> has a syntactic object in its subcategorization: <u>fell</u> [__NP].

Surface structure 表层结构

The syntactic representation of a sentence after all the **transformation**s have applied to the **deep structure**, before the application of the **phonological rules**. Also later called 'S-structure'.

Theta role 论旨角色

The generalized semantic roles that syntactic constituents take on, e.g. 'agent' for the doer of an action, 'theme' for the undergoer.

Trace 语迹

A proposal that a **movement rule** should leave a 'trace' of the moved constituent in the developing phrase structure.

Transformation 转换

A rule that operates in the generation of the **surface structure** of a sentence from its **deep structure**. For example, the 'passive' transformation would generate 'The tree was felled by the forester' from the kernel sentence 'The forester felled the tree'. Transformations disappeared from later versions of the theory.

Tree (diagram) 树（形图）

A usual way of diagramming the syntactic respresentations of a sentence in TGG. Trees contain 'nodes', from which descend 'daughters', more than one of which will be 'sisters'.

X-bar syntax X 阶标句法

The theory that all phrases have basically the same structure (XP), with 'X' standing for the head of the phrase (noun, verb, preposition, etc.). In a **tree** diagram, the node for a phrase would be 'N' (i.e. N-bar), and so on.

Dependency grammar 依存语法

Actant 行动元／题元

The obligatory dependent of a verb, usually representing the entities (persons, things) involved in the action or state denoted by the verb. For example, in 'Jane signed the document yesterday in black ink', <u>Jane</u> and <u>the document</u> are the actants. Compare **circonstant**.

Circonstant (circumstance) 状态元

The optional elements dependent on a verb, usually expressing notions of time, place, manner, reason, etc. For example, in 'Jane signed the document yesterday in black ink', <u>yesterday</u> and <u>in black ink</u> are the circonstants. Compare **actant**.

Dependent 从属词 / 依存词

An item that relates to a superordinate **governor**, such as the nouns <u>Jane</u> and <u>document</u> in 'Jane signed the document', which are the dependents of <u>sign</u>.

Facultative 可选的（从属词 / 依存词）

An item that is intermediate between **obligatory** and **optional**. For example, in 'The boys pushed the old pram into the river', the prepositional phrase of 'goal', <u>into the river</u>, is not obligatory for a sentence with the verb <u>push</u> to be grammatical (i.e. 'The boys pushed the pram' is grammatical); however, <u>push</u> does imply 'somewhere', and so <u>into the river</u> is more than optional. The term 'facultative' is used for such cases.

Governor 支配词

An item that has **dependents**, e.g. verbs. The number and types of dependent are specified by its **valency**.

Obligatory 必须的（从属词 / 依存词）

A dependent that must occur for the structure to be grammatical. **Actant**s are usually obligatory; a **circonstant** may sometimes be obligatory, e.g. the goal in a sentence with <u>put</u> ('She put the jars in the cupboard').

Optional 任选的（从属词 / 依存词）

A dependent that is not necessary for the structure to be grammatical. **Circonstant**s are usually optional, representing information (time, place, manner, etc.) that may or may not be expressed.

Valency 价 / 向

A term borrowed from chemistry to express the number of **actant**s that a verb takes; e.g. <u>smile</u> has a valency of 1, <u>kick</u> a valency of 2, and <u>tell</u> a valency of 3. The term's use has been extended to include both the type of syntactic elements and their general semantic features. For example, <u>smile</u> takes a Subject noun phrase that usually refers to a person; <u>tell</u> has a human Subject, a human Indirect Object, and a Direct Object that may be a noun (<u>the story</u>) or a prepositional phrase (<u>about the incident</u>) or a <u>that</u>-clause (<u>that he had a new job</u>).

Cognitive linguistics 认知语言学

Categorization 范畴化

This is fundamental to cognitive linguistics, rather than being rule-based like generative grammar. Categorization is variously based on prototypes, mental images, metaphor, etc.

Cognitive commitment 认知原则 / 认知承诺

One of the fundamentals of cognitive linguistics, that language is characterized in accordance with knowledge about the mind and brain from other disciplines. This also represents a limitation, as it is dependent on advances in knowledge from these other disciplines. See also **generalization commitment.**

Cognitive grammar 认知语法

This aims to model the language system, the 'mental grammar'. Meaning is seen as central to grammar, and language is not conceived as modular but as integrated.

Cognitive semantics 认知语义学

This looks at the relationship between experience, the conceptual system, and semantic structure as encoded in language. Meaning is seen as 'encyclopedic', and not merely in 'dictionary' terms.

Conceptual metaphor 概念隐喻

Thought is said to be fundamentally metaphorical. For example, 'quality' is assessed in terms of 'vertical elevation', by means of terms like high and low; life itself is conceived as a 'journey', which we <u>set out</u> on and <u>come to the end</u> of. See especially Lakoff & Johnson (2003).

Construction grammar 构式语法

Not a necessary part of cognitive linguistics, but developed from it; it aims to model grammar in terms of an inventory of constructions, rather than in terms of words and rules.

Embodied cognition 具身认知 / 体验认知

The idea that the way in which we perceive things is determined by the makeup of our bodies, including our neurological organization. For example, how we see colour is dependent on physical attributes.

Encyclopedic semantics 百科知识语义观

The meaning of a word is not encapsulated in a dictionary definition, but encompasses all kinds of knowledge that we have about the concept it expresses, so that mention of a word triggers a 'frame' or 'domain', with which the concept is associated.

Generalization commitment 普遍原则

Cognitive linguistics aims to investigate how aspects of linguistic knowledge emerge from a common set of human cognitive abilities; it is committed to making generalizations across as wide a range of phenomena as possible, not only within linguistics, but also in neighbouring cognitive disciplines. See also **cognitive commitment**.

Idealized cognitive model (ICM) 理想化认知模型

Relatively stable cognitive representations of theories about the world, by means of which we make conceptual sense of our experience and to which we relate it, including the interpretation of metaphor.

Image schema 意象图式

Prelinguistic structure of experience that enables conceptual metaphors to be mapped. For example, the image schema of 'container' enables understanding of many expressions with <u>in(to)</u> and <u>out</u> (<u>get into debt</u>, <u>come out of a coma</u>).

Mental space 心智空间

How we partition meaning into temporary regions or packets as we talk or think, which then have mappings between them, to enable our understanding and our uttering. They are structured by 'frames' and cognitive models.

Symbolic assembly/unit 符号集 / 符号单元

A form-meaning pairing, basic to cognitive linguistics; it is similar to Saussure's signifier/signified, though it is applied to all kinds of linguistic unit, not just words, and including constructions.

Key readings

Inevitably, the publications cited in this section will comprise a personal selection. They are intended to point you to further readings and deeper exploration of the terms and topics listed in this book; and they are mostly additional to the references given in the entries. They have been chosen because they are largely introductory in style and scope, they are mostly recently published (this century), and they are all in print as of April 2007. In general, they deal with linguistics, rather than with a particular language, but there are some publications that deal specifically with English. This section is organized under the headings that have been used earlier, with the addition of an initial 'general' heading. The section concludes with a list of the main journals in linguistics, again organized under the familiar headings; and each journal title is accompanied by its website address.

General

Encyclopedias that survey the discipline of linguistics:

Crystal, D. (1997) *The Cambridge Encyclopedia of Language*, Second Edition, Cambridge University Press.

Malmkjaer, K. (2004) (ed.) *The Linguistics Encyclopedia*, Second Revised Edition, Routledge.

Introductory textbooks:

Hall, C. J. (2005) *An Introduction to Language and Linguistics*, Continuum.

Yule, G. (2006) *The Study of Language*, Third Edition, Cambridge University Press.

Phonetics and phonology

Introductory textbooks:

Ashby, M. & Maidment, J. (2005) *Introducing Phonetic Science*, Cambridge University Press.

Gussenhoven, C. & Jacobs, H. (2005) *Understanding Phonology*, Second Edition, Hodder Arnold.

Ladefoged, P. (2004) *Vowels and Consonants*, Second Edition, Blackwell.

Phonetics and phonology of English:

Collins, B. S. & Mees, I. M. (2003) *Practical Phonetics and Phonology*, Routledge.

Roach, P. (2001) *English Phonetics and Phonology*, Third Edition, Cambridge University Press.

A classic account of British English pronunciation:

Cruttenden, A. (2001) (ed.) *Gimson's Pronunciation of English*, Sixth Edition, Hodder Arnold.

Grammar: morphology and syntax

Introductory textbooks:

Bauer, L. (2003) *Introducing Linguistic Morphology*, Second Edition, Edinburgh University Press.

Booij, G. (2005) *The Grammar of Words: An Introduction to Linguistic Morphology*, Oxford University Press.

Kroeger, P. R. (2005) *Analyzing Grammar: An introduction*, Cambridge

University Press.

Moravcsik, E. A. (2006) *An Introduction to Syntax*, Continuum.

Accounts of English morphology and syntax:

Carstairs-McCarthy, A. (2001) *An Introduction to English Morphology*, Edinburgh University Press.

Dixon, R. M. W. (2005) *A Semantic Approach to English Grammar*, Oxford University Press.

Huddleston, R. & Pullum, G. K. (2005) *A Student's Introduction to English Grammar*, Cambridge University Press.

Reference grammars of English:

Biber, D., Conrad, S. & Leech, G. (2002) *Longman's Student Grammar of Spoken and Written English*, Longman.

Carter, R. & McCarthy, M. (2006) *Cambridge Grammar of English*, Cambridge University Press.

Semantics and pragmatics

Introductory textbooks:

Grundy, P. (2000) *Doing Pragmatics*, Second Edition, Hodder Arnold.

Huang, Y. (2006) *Pragmatics*, Oxford University Press.

Loebner, S. (2002) *Understanding Semantics*, Hodder Arnold.

Saeed, J. I. (2003) *Semantics*, Second Edition, Blackwell.

Accounts of the semantics and pragmatics of English:

Griffiths, P. (2006) *An Introduction to English Semantics and Pragmatics*, Edinburgh University Press.

Jackson, H. & Zé Amvela, E. (2007) *Words, Meaning and Vocabulary*, Second Edition, Continuum.

An account of politeness:

Christie, C. (2007) *Linguistic Politeness Theories and applications*, Edinburgh University Press.

Discourse and text analysis

Introductory textbooks:

Johnstone, B. (2007) *Discourse Analysis: An Introduction*, Second Edition, Blackwell.

Martin, J. R & Rose, D. (2007) *Working with Discourse: Meaning Beyond the Clause*, Second Edition, Continuum.

An account of conversation analysis:

Ten Have, P. (2007) *Doing Conversation Analysis*, Second Edition, Sage.

An account of critical discourse analysis:

Fairclough, N. (2001) *Language and Power*, Second Edition, Longman.

Sociolinguistics

Introductory textbooks:

Holmes, J. (2001) *An Introduction to Sociolinguistics*, Second Edition, Longman.

Meyerhoff, M. (2006) *Introducing Sociolinguistics*, Routledge.

Wardhaugh, R. (2005) *An Introduction to Sociolinguistics*, Fifth Edition, Blackwell.

Specifically related to English:

Davies, D. (2005) *Varieties of Modern English: An Introduction*, Longman.

Hughes, A., Trudgill, P. & Watt, D. (2005) *English Accents and Dialects*, Fourth Edition, Hodder Arnold.

On language and gender:

Coates, J. (2004) *Women, Men and Language*, Third Edition, Longman.

Eckert, P. & McConnell-Ginet, S. (2003) *Language and Gender*, Cambridge University Press.

Psycholinguistics

Introductory textbooks:

Field, J. (2003) *Psycholinguistics*, Routledge.

Steinberg, D. D. & Sciarini, N. V. (2006) *An Introduction to Psycholinguistics*, Second Edition, Longman.

On the mental lexicon:

Aitchison, J. (2002) *Words in the Mind*, Third Edition, Blackwell.

On language acquisition and learning:

Cook, V. J. (2001) *Second Language Learning and Language Teaching*, Third Edition, Hodder Arnold.

Foley, J. & Thompson, L. (2003) *Language Learning: A Lifelong Process*, Hodder Arnold.

O'Grady, W. (2005) *How Children Learn Language*, Cambridge University Press.

Historical linguistics

Introductory textbooks:

Campbell, L. (2004) *Historical Linguistics: An Introduction*, Second Edition, Edinburgh University Press.

Hale, M. (2006) *Historical Linguistics: Theory and Method*, Blackwell.

Jones, M. & Singh, I. (2005) *Exploring Language Change*, Routledge.

On typology:

Song, J. J. (2000) *Linguistic Typology: Morphology and Syntax*, Longman.

On the history of English:

Beal, J. C. (2004) *English in Modern Times*, Hodder Arnold.

Mugglestone, L. (2006) (ed.) *The Oxford History of English*, Oxford University Press.

Singh, I. (2005) *The History of English: A Student's Guide*, Hodder Arnold.

Applied linguistics

Introductory textbooks:

Davies, A. (1999) *An Introduction to Applied Linguistics: From Practice to Theory*, Edinburgh University Press.

Schmitt, N. (2002) *An Introduction to Applied Linguistics*, Hodder Arnold.

On translation:

Bell, R. (1991) *On Translation and Translating: Theory and Practice*, Longman.

Hatim, B. & Munday, J. (2004) *Translation*, Routledge.

On lexicography:

Jackson, H. (2002) *Lexicography: An Introduction*, Routledge.

On forensic linguistics:

Gibbons, J. (2003) *Forensic Linguistics: An Introduction to Language in the Justice System*, Blackwell.

Olsson, J. (2004) *Forensic Linguistics: An Introduction to Language, Crime and the Law*, Continuum.

On speech and language therapy:

Black, M. & Chiat, S. (2003) *Linguistics for Clinicians*, Hodder Arnold.

Crystal, D. & Varley, R. (1998) *Introduction to Language Pathology*, Fourth Edition, Whurr.

On literacy:

Holme, R. (2004) *Literacy: An Introduction*, Edinburgh University Press.

On language and ecology:

Fill, A. & Mühlhäusler, P. (2006) (eds) *Ecolinguistics Reader*, Continuum.

Stylistics

Introductory textbooks:

Simpson, P. (2004) *Stylistics*, Routledge.

Toolan, M. (1998) *Language in Literature: An Introduction to Stylistics*, Hodder Arnold.

Verdonk, P. (2002) *Stylistics*, Oxford University Press.

An explanation of terms:

Wales, K. (2001) *A Dictionary of Stylistics*, Second Edition, Longman.

Corpus linguistics

Introductory textbooks:

McEnery, T. & Wilson, A. (2001) *Corpus Linguistics*, Second Edition, Edinburgh University Press.

Teubert, W. & Cermáková, A. (2007) *Corpus Linguistics: A Short Introduction*, Continuum.

A volume of classic articles:

Sampson, G. & McCarthy, D. (2005) (eds) *Corpus Linguistics: Readings in a Widening Discipline*, Continuum.

Schools of linguistics

General:

Allan, K. (2007) *The Western Classical Tradition in Linguistics*, Equinox.

Chapman, S. & Routledge, C. (2005) (eds) *Key Thinkers in Linguistics and the Philosophy of Language*, Edinburgh University Press.

Robins, R. H. (1997) *A Short History of Linguistics*, Fourth Edition, Longman.

On structuralism:

Harris, R. (2003) *Saussure and his Interpreters*, Second Edition, Edinburgh

University Press.

On systemic-functional linguistics:

Eggins, S. (2004) *An Introduction to Systemic Functional Linguistics*, Second Edition, Continuum.

Thompson, G. (2004) *Introducing Functional Grammar*, Second Edition, Hodder Arnold.

On transformational-generative grammar:

Cook, V. & Newson, N. (2007) *Chomsky's Universal Grammar*, Third Edition, Blackwell.

Smith, N. (2004) *Chomsky: Ideas and Ideals*, Second Edition, Cambridge University Press.

On dependency grammar:

Cornell, A., Fischer, K. & Roe, I. F. (2003) *Valency in Practice: Valenz in der Praxis*, Peter Lang.

Mel'čuk, I. A. (1988) *Dependency Syntax: Theory and Practice*, State University of New York Press.

On cognitive linguistics:

Evans, V. & Green, M. (2006) *Cognitive Linguistics: An Introduction*, Edinburgh University Press.

Ungerer, F. & Schmid, H. J. (2006) *An Introduction to Cognitive Linguistics*, Second Edition, Longman.

Journals

General:

Journal of Linguistics (http://journals.cambridge.org/dction/displayJournal?jid =LIN)

Language (www.lsadc.org/info/pubs-language.cfm)

Folia Linguistica (www.degruyter.de/rs/384_388_ENU_h.htm)

Journal of English Linguistics (http://eng.sagepub.com/)

English Language and Linguistics (http://journals.cambridge.org/action/
displayJournal?jid = ELL)

Phonetics and phonology:

Journal of Phonetics (www.elsevier.com/wps/find/journaldescription.
cws_home/622896/description#description)

Journal of the International Phonetic Association (http://journals.
cambridge.org/action/displayJournal?jid = IPA)

Phonology (http://journals.cambridge.org/action/displayJournal?jid =
PHO)

Grammar: morphology and syntax:

Morphology (www.springer.com/journal/11525)

Syntax (www.blackwellpublishing.com/journal.asp?ref = 1368-0005)

Semantics and pragmatics:

Journal of Semantics (http://jos.oxfordjournals.org/)

Journal of Pragmatics (www.elsevier.com/wps/find/journaldescription.
cws_home/505593/description#description)

Discourse and text analysis:

Discourse Studies (www.sagepub.com/journalsProdDesc.nav?prodld =
Journal200865)

Text and Talk (www.degruyter.de/rs/384_410_DEU_h.htm)

Sociolinguistics:

International Journal of the Sociology of Language (www.degruyter.de/
rs/384_403_ENU_h.htm)

Language in Society (http://journals.cambridge.org/action/displayJournal?-
jid=LSY)

Journal of Sociolinguistics (www.blackwellpublishing.com/journal.
asp?ref = 1360-6441)

Psycholinguistics:

Applied Psycholinguistics (www.cambridge.org/journals/journal_catalogue.asp?mnemonic=APS)

Journal of Psycholinguistic Research (www.springer.com/west/home/linguistics? SGWID = 4-40369-70-35608584-0)

Historical linguistics:

Diachronica (www.benjamins.nl/cgi-bin/t_seriesview.cgi?series = DIA)

Folia Linguistica Historica (www.degruyter.de/r5/384_388_ENU_h.htm)

Applied linguistics:

Applied Linguistics (http://applij.oxfordjournals.org/)

International Journal of Applied Linguistics (www.blackwellpublishing.com/journal.asp?ref = 0802-6106)

Journal of Applied Linguistics (www.equinoxjournals.com/ojs/index.php/JAL)

Stylistics:

Style (www.engl.niu.edu/style/)

Language and Literature (www.sagepub.co.uk/journalsProdDesc.nav?prodld = Journal200860)

Corpus linguistics:

International Journal of Corpus Linguistics (www.benjamins.com/cgi-bin/t_seriesview.cgi?series = IJCL)

Corpora (www.eup.ed.ac.uk/journals/content.aspx?pageld = 1&journalld = 12801)

References

Allerton, D. J. (1982) *Valency and the English Verb*, Academic Press.

Beaugrande, R. de & Dressier, W. V. (1981) *Introduction to Text Linguistics*, Longman.

Brown, P. & Levinson, S. (1987) *Politeness: Some Universals in Language Usage*, Cambridge University Press.

Carter, R. & McCarthy, M. (1997) *Exploring Spoken English*, Cambridge University Press.

Coates, J. (1983) *The Semantics of the Modal Auxiliaries*, Croom Helm.

Coulthard, M. (1985) *An Introduction to Discourse Analysis*, 2nd Edition, Longman.

Croft, W. & Cruse, D. A. (2004) *Cognitive Linguistics*, Cambridge University Press.

Cruse, D. A. (1986) *Lexical Semantics*, Cambridge University Press.

Eggins, S. (2004) *An Introduction to Systemic Functional Linguistics*, Continuum.

Fairclough, N. (1995) *Critical Discourse Analysis*, Longman.

Fillmore, C. J. (1987) *Fillmore's Case Grammar*, Julius Groos.

Fischer, K. (2003) (ed.) *Valency in Practice*, Peter Lang.

Fries, C. C. (1952) *The Structure of English,* Harcourt Brace & Co.

Gardner, R. C. & Lambert, W. E. (1972), *Attitudes and Motivation in Second Language Learning*, Newbury House.

Givón, T. (1993) *English Grammar: a Function-based Introduction*, John Benjamins.

Halliday, M. A. K. (1973) *Explorations in the Functions of Language*, Edward Arnold.

Halliday, M. A. K. & Hasan, R. (1976) *Cohesion in English*, Longman.

Halliday, M. A. K. & Matthiessen, C. (2004) *An Introduction to Functional Grammar*, Third Edition, Hodder Arnold.

Hartmann, R. R. K. & James, G. (2001) *Dictionary of Lexicography*, Routledge.

Herbst, T., Heath, D., Rose, I. F. & Götz, D. (2004) *A Valency Dictionary of English*, Mouton de Gruyter.

Hockett, C. F. (1966) 'The problem of universals in language', in Greenberg, J. H. *Universals of Language*, 2nd edn, MIT Press, pp. 1-29.

Hoey, M. (1983) *On the Surface of Discourse*, Allen & Unwin.

— (2005) *Lexical Priming*, Routledge.

Hudson, R. (2007) *Language Networks: The New Word Grammar*, Oxford University Press.

Hunston, S. & Thompson, G. (2000) (eds) *Evaluation in Text: Authorial Stance and the Construction of Discourse*, Oxford University Press.

Hutchby, I. & Wooffitt, R. (1988) *Conversation Analysis*, Polity Press.

James, C. (1980) *Contrastive Analysis*, Longman.

—(1998) *Errors in Language Learning and Use: Exploring Error Analysis*, Longman.

Jones, D. (1917) *English Pronouncing Dictionary*, (17th edition, 2006, Cambridge University Press).

Joseph, J., Love, N. & Taylor, T. (2001) *Landmarks in Linguistic Thought II: the Western Tradition in the Twentieth Century*, Routledge.

Lakoff, G. & Johnson, M. (2003) *Metaphors We Live By*, 2nd Edition, University of Chicago Press.

Leech, G. N. (1972) *Meaning and the English Verb*, Longman.

McEnery, T. & Wilson, A. (2001) *Corpus Linguistics: An Introduction*, 2nd Edition, Edinburgh University Press.

Mitchell, R. & Myles, F. (2006) *Second Language Learning Theories*, 2nd Edition, Hodder Arnold.

Olsson, J. (2004) *Forensic Linguistics: An Introduction to Language, Crime and the Law*, Continuum.

Palmer, F. R. (1988) *The English Verb*, Longman.

—(1990) *Modality and the English Modals*, 2nd Edition, Longman.

Roach, P. (2000) *English Phonetics and Phonology*, 3rd Edition, Cambridge University Press.

Rosch, E. (1983) 'Prototype classification and logical classification: the two systems', in Scholnick, E. F. (ed.) *New Trends in Conceptual Representation: Challenges to Piaget's Theory?*, Erlbaum.

Ryan, E. B. & Giles, H. (1982) (eds) *Attitudes to Language Variation*, Edward Arnold.

Smith, N. (1999) *Chomsky: Ideas and Ideals,* Cambridge University Press.

Stenström, A. B. (1994) *An Introduction to Spoken Interaction*, Longman.

Toolan, M. J. (2001) *Narrative: A Critical Linguistic Introduction*, 2nd Edition, Routledge.

Wales, K. (2001) *A Dictionary of Stylistics*, 2nd Edition, Longman.

Werlich, E. (1976) *A Text Grammar of English*, Quelle & Meyer.

Index